Samuel Johnson, I. P. Fleming

London

And, The Vanity of Human Wishes. Sixth Edition

Samuel Johnson, I. P. Fleming

London
And, The Vanity of Human Wishes. Sixth Edition

ISBN/EAN: 9783337176662

Printed in Europe, USA, Canada, Australia, Japan

Cover: Foto ©ninafisch / pixelio.de

More available books at **www.hansebooks.com**

Dr Johnson's Satires

LONDON

AND

THE VANITY OF HUMAN WISHES

WITH

NOTES, HISTORICAL & BIOGRAPHICAL, & a GLOSSARY

BY

I. P. FLEMING, M.A., D.C.L.

AUTHOR OF 'ANALYSIS OF BACON'S ADVANCEMENT OF LEARNING,
WITH A COMPLETE COURSE OF EXAMINATION-QUESTIONS'
MILTON'S 'SAMSON AGONISTES' ETC.

SIXTH EDITION

LONDON

LONGMANS, GREEN, AND CO.
AND NEW YORK: 15 EAST 16th STREET
1890

LONDON

AND

THE VANITY OF HUMAN WISHES

PRINTED BY
SPOTTISWOODE AND CO., NEW-STREET SQUARE
LONDON

CONTENTS.

The text adopted in the following pages is taken from the Edition of JOHNSON'S *Works by* Sir JOHN HAWKINS, 1787.

DR JOHNSON'S SATIRES.

——◦◦——

INTRODUCTION.

THE most striking figure in the social and literary history
of the period from 1709 to 1784 was that of SAMUEL
JOHNSON. His career was preeminently that of a man of
letters ; and the slow and laborious efforts by which, in
spite of every obstacle, personal as well as material, he
raised himself to the highest intellectual supremacy,
present a spectacle equally instructive to us and honour-
able to him. He was born in 1709, the son of a learned
but poor and struggling provincial bookseller in Lichfield ; and he exhibited, from his very childhood, the same
singular union of mental power and constitutional indo-
lence, ambition and hypochondriacal gloom, which distinguished him through life. He was disfigured and half
blinded by a scrofulous disorder, which scarred and
deformed a face and figure naturally imposing, and at
the same time afflicted him with strange and involuntary
contortions, reacting also upon his mind and temper, and
making him sombre, despondent, and irritable. In the

B

various humble seminaries where he received his early education, he unfailingly took the first place ; and being assisted by a benevolent patron with the means of studying at the University, he carried to Pembroke College, Oxford, an amount of scholarship very rare at his age. Here he remained about three years, remarkable for the roughness and uncouthness of his manners, and no less for his wit and insubordination, as well as for that sturdy spirit of independence, which made him reject with indignation any offer of assistance. The story of his throwing away a pair of new shoes, which some one pitying the poverty of the ragged student had placed at his door, is striking, and even pathetic. His father's affairs being in hopeless confusion, and the promises of assistance not being fulfilled, he was obliged to leave the University without a degree ; and receiving at his father's death only 20*l.* as his share of the inheritance, he abandoned it to his mother's use, for he was ever a most dutiful and generous son, and entered upon the hard career of teacher and usher in various provincial schools. For success in this profession he was equally unfitted by his person, his nature, and the peculiar character of his mind and acquirements, and after unsuccessfully attempting to keep a school himself at Edial, near Lichfield, he began that tremendous struggle with labour and want which continued during thirty years.

His first literary undertaking was a translation of FATHER LOBO'S ' Travels in Abyssinia' ; but his hopes of success meeting with little but disappointment, he determined to launch upon the great ocean of London literary life. In 1736 he had married Mrs. PORTER, a widow, old enough to be his mother, but whom, notwithstanding her defects of person and cultivation, he always loved with the energy of his masculine and affectionate character. In 1737 he travelled to London in company with DAVID GARRICK, one of the few pupils he had under his charge at Edial, who was destined in another path to follow a brilliant career. GARRICK'S ambition was to appear on the stage, where he speedily took the first place ; and JOHNSON carried with him the unfinished MS. of his tragedy *Irene*, without fortune, without friends, of singularly uncouth and forbidding exterior. JOHNSON entered upon the career—then perhaps at its lowest ebb of profit and respectability—of a bookseller's hack or literary drudge. He became a contributor to divers journals, and particularly to the 'Gentleman's Magazine,' then carried on by its founder CAVE ; and as an obscure labourer for the press, he furnished criticisms, prefaces, translations, in short all kinds of humble literary work, and ultimately supplied reports of the proceedings in Parliament, though the names of the speakers, in obedience to the law which then rendered it penal to reproduce the debates, were disguised under imaginary titles.

He first emerged into popularity in 1738 by the publication of his satire entitled ' London,'—an admirable paraphrase or reproduction of the *Third* Satire of JUVENAL ; in which he adapts the sentiments and topics of the great Roman poet to the neglect of letters in London, and the humiliations which an honest man must encounter in a society where foreign quacks and native scoundrels could alone hope for success. During this miserable and obscure portion of his career, when he dined in a cellar upon six pennyworth of meat and a pennyworth of bread, when he signed himself in a note to his employer ' Yours *impransus*, S. JOHNSON,' when his ragged coat and torn shoes made him ashamed to appear at the table of his publisher, and caused him to devour his dinner behind a screen, he retained all his native dignity of mind and severe honesty of principle. There is something affecting in the picture of this great and noble mind labouring on through toil and distress which would have crushed most men, and which, though it roughened his manners, only intensified his humanity and augmented his self-respect.

In 1744 he published his ' Life of Savage,' that unhappy poet whose career was so extraordinary, and whose vices were not less striking than his talents. JOHNSON had known him well, and they had often wandered supperless and homeless about the streets at midnight. The vigorous and manly thought expressed in JOHNSON'S sonorous language rendered this biography popular ; but the improvement in the author's circumstances was very tardy in making its appearance : no literary life was ever a more correct exemplification than that of JOHNSON of the truth of his own majestic line—

Slow rises worth, by poverty depressed.

During the eight years extending from 1747 to 1755 JOHNSON was engaged in the execution of his laborious undertaking, the compilation of his great ' Dictionary of the English Language,' which long occupied the place among us of the Dictionary of the Academy in France and Spain.

While engaged in this laborious task he diverted his mind by the publication of the 'Vanity of Human Wishes,' a companion to his 'London,' being a similar imitation of the *Tenth* Satire of his Roman prototype. This is written in a loftier, more solemn, and declamatory style than the preceding poem, and is a fine specimen of JOHNSON'S dignified but somewhat gloomy rhetoric. The illustrations drawn from history of the futility of those objects which men sigh for—literary, military, or political renown, beauty, wealth, long life, or splendid alliances, JOHNSON has reproduced with kindred vigour ; but he has added several of his own, where he shows a power and grandeur in no sense inferior to that of JUVENAL. Thus to the striking picture of the fate of SÈJANUS, related with such grim humour by the Roman satirist, JOHNSON has added the not less impressive picture of the disgrace of WOLSEY ; and his episode of CHARLES XII. is no unworthy counterpart to the portrait of HANNIBAL (Shaw's ' Outlines of Literature ').

(2.) JOHNSON AND JUVENAL COMPARED.

Our readers may not perhaps know that the Third Satire of JUVENAL is directed against the corruptions of society in Rome, against the miseries and humiliations which a residence in the great city imposes upon a poor but virtuous man, and the immense riches and influence obtained by the most unworthy arts by Greeks and favourite freedmen. The picture is a striking and impressive one, and has lost none of its grandeur in the hands of the English copyist, who has with consummate skill transferred the invectives of JUVENAL to the passion for imitating French fashions, and adapted the images of JUVENAL to London vices, discomforts, and corruptions.

In the Tenth Satire (perhaps the grandest specimen which we possess of this kind of writing) the Roman takes a higher ground, and in an uninterrupted torrent of noble eloquence has pointed out the folly and emptiness of all other objects which form the chief aim of human desires. He shows us successively the misery which has accompanied, and the ruin which has followed, the possession of those advantages for which men sigh and pray ; he exhibits the vanity of riches, ambition, eloquence, military glory, long life, and beauty, the whole exemplified by the most signal examples drawn from history of the folly of human hopes :

Magnaque numinibus Diis exaudita malignis.

Many passages of JOHNSON'S Satires must be regarded as translations—consummate translations—of the words of JUVENAL; but he frequently changes, augments, and strengthens : as, for example, JUVENAL has instanced SEJANUS as a proof of the unstability of political power and the favour of the great. JOHNSON has added to this impressive picture the fall of WOLSEY. HANNIBAL, and ALEXANDER—whose death forms so instructive a moral of the folly of the conqueror and general—are not excluded ; but the equally warning story of CHARLES XII. is made the vehicle for a moral lesson not less admirably expressed, and even more impressive, from its nearness of time, to a modern reader. The lofty philosophical tone of gloomy eloquence perhaps is even more uniformly sustained in the English than in the Roman poet ; and in the con-clusion of the Satire, where, after showing the nothingness of all earthly hopes, the voice of reason points out what are the only objects worthy of the wise man's desire— health, innocence, resignation, and tranquillity—the En-glish poet must be allowed to have surpassed in pathetic solemnity even the grandeur of his model, so far as the consolatory truths of Christian revelation are sublimer than the imperfect lights of Stoic paganism.

(3.) THE STYLE AND CHARACTER OF JOHNSON'S SATIRES.

(i.) 'LONDON.

As a general satire this poem is admitted to be one of the finest productions in the English language. It was originally published anonymously, but its merit is so conspicuous that it reached a second edition in a single week, and at once stamped its author with the reputation of a man of genius. The biographers of JOHNSON state that he was then living in a sort of literary obscurity, as a mere contributor to the 'Gentleman's Magazine,' and when he offered the poem to Mr. CAVE the publisher, it was 'to dispose of for the benefit of the author under very disadvantageous circumstances of fortune.' CAVE, say they, who had so much distinguished himself by his generous encouragement of poetry, communicated it to DODSLEY, the bookseller, who had taste enough to perceive its merit, and who agreed to give ten guineas for the copyright,—a sum utterly disproportioned to the author's labour and ingenuity, but he was actually in such distress that the small profit which so short a poem could yield was counted as a relief and received with gratitude.

It came out on the same morning with POPE'S satire, entitled ' 1738,' and the general enquiry was, Who can be the author ? LYTTLETON, the instant it appeared, carried it in raptures to POPE, who then filled the poetical throne without a rival, and who was so struck with its merit that he sought to discover the author. ' Whoever he is,' said he, ' he will soon be *deterré.*' Future events verified the prognostication, and JOHNSON came afterwards to be in the literary world, what POPE then was, ' lord of the ascendant.'

The poem of ' London' breathes the true vehement and contemptuous indignation of its Roman prototype, the Third Satire of JUVENAL. It blazes forth with original fire in the liveliness of its correspondent allusions, the energy of its expressions, and the frequency of its apostrophes. Sometimes, however, the English poet takes from the Roman nothing more than the subject, proving or illustrating it according to the originality of his own conceptions, or the warmth of his own fancy, and sometimes in the true spirit of independent genius and power he deserts him altogether ; for it is not only where the modesty of an

English ear and the inapplicability of the original to modern customs require it, that he does so, but it is in places where the topics and the moral use are applicable to modern London as they are to ancient Rome. BOILEAU has imitated the same Satire with great success, applying it to *Paris,* as JOHNSON applied it to London; but it is generally admitted in a comparison of the two poems that the latter bears away the palm.

(ii.) 'THE VANITY OF HUMAN WISHES.'

In January 1749, eleven years after the publication of his 'London,' Dr. JOHNSON gave to the world this second imitation of the Roman Satirist with his name. Though his reputation as an author had in the interval been progressively advancing, yet he got from DODSLEY only fifteen guineas for the copyright with a reservation to print one edition for his own behoof.

This production, generally speaking, is not equal as a whole to his poem on London, but in some particulars it may be considered superior. It has less of common life and the exaggeration of party spirit—more of philosophic dignity and sublime morality, and from beginning to end there is a nearer approximation to the lofty and energetic tone of the great Roman original. Indeed, it has been said by some that it challenges comparison with JUVENAL in every line, and in several instances it only professes to be a paraphrase.

In the original the Roman poet has taken his subject from the second *Alcibiades* of PLATO, and intermixes various sentiments of SOCRATES concerning the object of prayers offered up to the Deity.   The general proposition is that good and evil are so little understood by mankind that their wishes, when granted, are always destructive. This is exemplified in a variety of instances such as riches, state preferment, eloquence, military glory, long life, and beauty.   For the characters which JUVENAL has chosen to illustrate his doctrine JOHNSON has substituted others from modern history.   Owing to the dearth of great modern examples, JOHNSON has fewer characters than the Roman Satirist; but in the aptness of his allusions and the happiness of his parallels he has succeeded wonderfully ; and though in strict truth it can hardly be said that he has surpassed his prototype, yet he has supported the competition nobly, and given to his translation all the air of an original. The ' Vanity of Human Wishes' is, without doubt, as high an effort of ethic poetry as any language can show.

(4.) THE PUBLICATION AND RECEPTION OF JOHNSON'S SATIRES.

What first displayed JOHNSON'S transcendent powers, and 'gave the world assurance of the man,' was his ' LONDON,' a poem in imitation of the *Third* Satire of JUVENAL, which came out in May 1738, and burst forth with a splendour, the rays of which will for ever encircle his name.   BOILEAU had imitated the same Satire with great success, applying it to *Paris* ; but an attentive comparison will satisfy every reader that he is much excelled by the English Juvenal. OLDHAM had also imitated it, and applied it to London, all which performances concur to prove, that great cities in every age and in every country will furnish similar topics of satire. Whether JOHNSON had previously read OLDHAM'S imitation I do not know ; but it is not a little remarkable that there is scarcely any coincidence found between the two performances though upon the very same subject. The only instances are, in describing ' London,' as the *sink* of foreign worthlessness :

the *common sewer*
Where France does all her filth and ordure pour.

OLDHAM.

The *common sewer* of Paris and of Rome.

JOHNSON.

And,

No calling or profession comes amiss,
A *needy monsieur* can be what he please.

OLDHAM.

All sciences a *fasting monsieur* knows.

JOHNSON.

The particulars which OLDHAM had collected, both as exhibiting the horrors of London, and of the times contrasted with better days, are different from those of JOHNSON, and in general well chosen, and well expressed.

There are, in OLDHAM'S imitation, many prosaic verses and bad rhymes, and his poem sets out with a strange inadvertent blunder :—

Tho' much concerned to *leave* my dear old friend,
I must, however, *his* design commend
Of fixing in the country.

It is plain he was not going to *leave his friend ;* his friend was *going to leave him.* A young lady once corrected this with good critical sagacity, to

Tho' much concerned to *lose* my dear old friend.

There is one passage in the original better transfused by OLDHAM than by JOHNSON :

Nil habet infelix paupertas durius in se
Quam quod ridiculos homines facit—

which is an exquisite remark on the galling meanness and contempt annexed to poverty : JOHNSON'S imitation is,

Of all the griefs that harass the distress'd,
Sure the most bitter is a scornful jest.

OLDHAM'S, though less elegant, is more just :

Nothing in poverty so ill is borne
As its exposing men to grinning scorn.

Where or in what manner this poem was composed, I am sorry that I neglected to ascertain with precision from JOHNSON'S own authority. He has marked upon his corrected copy of the first edition of it 'written in 1738 ; ' and, as it was published in the month of May in that year, it is evident that much time was not employed in preparing it for the press.

To us who have long known the manly force, bold spirit, and masterly versification of this poem, it is a matter of curiosity to observe the diffidence with which its author brought it forward into public notice, while he is so cautious as not to avow it to be his own production ; and with what humility he offers to allow the printer to

alter any stroke of satire which he might dislike. That
any such alteration was made we do not know. If we
did, we could not but feel an indignant regret ; but how
painful is it to see that a writer of such vigorous powers
of mind was actually in such distress, that the small
profit which so short a poem, however excellent, could
yield was courted as a 'relief' !

It has been generally said, I know not with what truth,
that JOHNSON offered his ' London to several booksellers,
none of whom would purchase it. To this circumstance
Mr. DERRICK alludes in the following lines of his ' Fortune,
a Rhapsody : '

> Will no kind patron Johnson own ?
> Shall Johnson friendless range the town ?
> And every publisher refuse
> The offspring of his happy Muse ?

But we have seen that the worthy, modest, and ingenious Mr. ROBERT DODSLEY had taste enough to
perceive its uncommon merit, and thought it creditable
to take a share in it. The fact is, that at a future con-
ference he bargained for the whole property of it, for which
he gave JOHNSON ten guineas ; who told me ' I might
perhaps have accepted less ; but that PAUL WHITEHEAD
a little before got ten guineas for a poem, and I would
not take less than PAUL WHITEHEAD.'

I may here observe that JOHNSON appeared to me to
undervalue PAUL WHITEHEAD upon every occasion
when he was mentioned, and, in my opinion, did not do
him justice ; but when it is considered that PAUL
WHITEHEAD was a member of a riotous and profane

club, we may account for JOHNSON having a prejudice
against him. PAUL WHITEHEAD was, indeed unfortunate in being not only slighted by JOHNSON, but violently
attacked by CHURCHILL, who utters the following impre-
cation :

> May I (can worse disgrace on manhood fall ?)
> Be born a Whitehead, and baptised a Paul.

Yet I shall never be persuaded to think meanly of the
author of so brilliant and pointed a satire as 'Manners.'

JOHNSON'S ' London' was published in May 1738, and
it is remarkable that it came out on the same morning
with POPE'S satire called ' 1738,' so that England had at
once its JUVENAL and HORACE as poetical monitors.
The Rev. Dr. DOUGLAS, Bishop of Salisbury, to whom I
am indebted for some obliging communications, was then
a student at Oxford, and remembers well the effect which
'London' produced. Everybody was delighted with it,
and there being no name to it, the first buzz of the literary
circle was 'there is an unknown poet, greater even than
POPE.' And it is recorded in the 'Gentleman's Magazine'
of that year, that it got to the second edition in the course
of a week.

One of the warmest patrons of this poem on its first
appearance was General OGLETHORPE, whose strong ' benevolence of soul' was unabated during the course of a
long life : though it is painful to think that he had too
much reason to become cold and callous, and discontented
with the world, from the neglect which he experienced
of his public and private worth by those in whose power
it was to gratify so gallant a veteran with marks of dis-

tinction. This extraordinary person was as remarkable, for his learning and taste as for his other eminent qualities ; and no man was more prompt, active, and generous, in encouraging merit. I have heard JOHNSON gratefully acknowledge in his presence the kind and effectual sup-, port which he gave to his ' London,' though unacquainted with its author.

POPE, who then filled the poetical throne without a rival, it may reasonably be presumed, must have been particularly struck by the sudden appearance of such a poet ; and, to his credit, let it be remembered, that his feelings and conduct on the occasion were candid and liberal. He requested Mr. RICHARDSON, son of the painter, to endeavour to find out who this new author was. Mr. RICHARDSON, after some inquiry, having informed him that he had discovered only that his name was JOHN-SON, and that he was some obscure man, POPE said ' He will soon be *déterré.*' We shall presently see from a note written by POPE that he was himself afterwards more successful in his inquiries than his friend.

That in this justly celebrated poem may be found a few rhymes which the critical position of English prosody at this day would disallow cannot be denied ; but with this small imperfection, which in the general blaze of its excellence is not perceived, it is, undoubtedly, one of the noblest productions in our language both for sentiment and expression. The nation was then in a ferment against the Court and the Ministry, which some years afterwards ended in the downfall of SIR ROBERT WALPOLE ; and it has been said that Tories are Whigs when out of place, and

Whigs Tories when in place ; so, as a Whig administration ruled with what force it could, a Tory opposition had
all the animation and all the eloquence of resistance to
power, aided by the common topics of patriotism, liberty
and independence.   Accordingly we find in JOHNSON'S
'London' the most spirited invectives against tyranny and
oppression, the warmest predilection for his own country
and the purest love of virtue ; interspersed with traits of
his own particular character and situation, not omitting
his prejudices as a true-born Englishman, not only against
foreign countries, but against Ireland and Scotland.   On
some of these topics I shall quote a few passages.

> The cheated nation's happy fav'rites, see !
> Mark whom the great caress, who frown on me !
>
> Has Heaven reserved, in pity to the poor,
> No pathless waste, or undiscover'd shore ?
> No secret island in the boundless main ?
> No peaceful desert yet unclaim'd by Spain ?
> Quick let us rise, the happy seats explore,
> And bear Oppression's insolence no more !
>
> How, when competitors like these contend,
> Can *surly Virtue* hope to fix a friend ?
>
> This mournful truth is everywhere confess'd,
> SLOW RISES WORTH, BY POVERTY DEPRESSED.

We may easily conceive with what feeling a great
mind like his, cramped and galled by narrow circumstances uttered this last line, which he marked by capitals.
The whole of the poem is eminently excellent ; and there
are in it such proofs of a knowledge of the world and of a
mature acquaintance with life, as cannot be contemplated

without wonder, when we consider that he was then only
in his twenty-ninth year, and had yet been so little in the
' busy haunts of men.'

Yet while we admire the poetical excellence of this
poem, candour obliges us to allow that the flame of
patriotism and zeal for popular resistance with which
it is fraught had no *just cause.* There was in truth *no*
' oppression;' the nation was *not* 'cheated.' Sir ROBERT
WALPOLE was a wise and benevolent minister, who thought
that the happiness and prosperity of a commercial country like ours would be best promoted by peace, which he
accordingly maintained with credit during a very long
period. JOHNSON himself afterwards (Oct. 21, 1773)
honestly acknowledged the merit of WALPOLE, whom he
called a 'fixed star :' while he characterised his opponent,
PITT, as 'a meteor.' But JOHNSON'S juvenile poem was
naturally impregnated with the fire of opposition, and
upon every account was universally admired.

BOSWELL'S Life of Johnson, ch. iii.

(ii.)

In January 1749 JOHNSON published the ' Vanity of
Human Wishes,'being the *Tenth* Satire of Juvenal imitated.
He, I believe, composed it the preceding year. Mrs.
JOHNSON, for the sake of country air, had lodgings at
Hampstead, to which he resorted occasionally, and there
the greatest part, if not the whole of the ' Imitation ' was
written. The fervid rapidity with which it was produced
is scarcely credible, I have heard him say that he com-

C

posed seventy lines of it in one day, without putting one
of them upon paper until they were finished. I remember
when I once regretted to him that he had not given to us
more of JUVENAL'S Satires, he said that he probably
should give more, for he had them all in his head ; by
which I understood that he had the originals and correspondent allusions floating in his mind, which he could,
when he pleased, embody and render permanent without
much labour.   Some of them, however, he observed,
were too gross for imitation.

The profits of a single poem, however excellent, appear
to have been very small in the last reign, compared with
what a publication of the same size has since been known
to yield.   I have mentioned, upon JOHNSON'S own authority, that for his ' London ' he had only ten guineas ;
and now, after his fame was established, he got for his
' Vanity of Human Wishes ' but five guineas more, as
is proved by an authentic document in my possession.

It will be observed that he reserves to himself the right
of printing one edition of this Satire, which was his prac-
tice upon occasion of the sale of all his writings, it being
his fixed intention to publish at some other period for his
own profit a complete collection of his works.

His ' Vanity of Human Wishes ' has less of common
life, but more of philosophic dignity, than his ' London.'
More readers therefore will be delighted with the pointed
style of ' London ' than with the *profound reflection* of the
' Vanity of Human Wishes.'   GARRICK, for instance, observed, in his sprightly manner—with more vivacity than
regard to just discrimination, as is usual with wits—' when

JOHNSON lived much with the HERVEYS, and saw a good ⟋˄˅
deal of what was passing in life, he wrote his " London,"
which is lively and easy.   When he became more retired,
he gave us his "Vanity of Human Wishes," which is as
hard as Greek. Had he gone on to imitate another Satire,
it would have been as hard as Hebrew.'

But the 'Vanity of Human Wishes' is, in the opinion
of the best judges, as high an effort of ethic poetry as any
language can show. The instances of variety of disappointment are chosen so judiciously and painted so
strongly, that the moment they are read they bring conviction to every thinking mind. That of the scholar must
have depressed the too sanguine expectations of many an
ambitious student.   That of the warrior CHARLES of
SWEDEN is, I think, as highly finished a picture as can
possibly be conceived. Were all the other excellencies
of this poem annihilated, it must ever have our grateful
reverence from its noble conclusion ; in which we are
consoled with the assurance that happiness may be at-
tained if we ' *apply our hearts* ' *to piety.*

BOSWELL'S *Life of Johnson*, ch. vi.

(5.) JUVENAL, DRYDEN, AND JOHNSON

The student should read along with JOHNSON'S adap-
tations of the *Third* and *Tenth* Satires of JUVENAL to the
state of London in his own days, DRYDEN'S translations
of the same Satires.   By way of assisting his comparison,
the chief points of resemblance are noted along with the
text.

(i.) ' LONDON.'

This being an adaptation of the *Third* Satire of JUVENAL, the argument which prefaces DRYDEN'S translation will explain the appositeness of JOHNSON'S application of the theme to London.

ARGUMENT OF THE THIRD SATIRE OF JUVENAL.

The story of this Satire speaks itself. UMBRITIUS, the SUPPOSED friend of JUVENAL, and himself a poet, is leaving Rome, and retiring to Cumæ. Our author accompanies him out of town. Before they take leave of each other, UMBRITIUS tells his friend the reasons which oblige him to lead a private life in an obscure place. He complains that an honest man cannot get his bread at Rome. That none but flatterers make their bread there —that Grecians and other foreigners raise themselves by those sordid arts which he describes, and against which he bitterly inveighs. He reckons up the several inconveniences which arise from city life, and the many dangers which attend it—upbraids the nobles for covetousness, for not rewarding good poets, and arraigns the government for starving them. The great art of the Satire is particularly shown in common places, and drawing in as many vices as could naturally fall into the compass of it.

(ii.) 'THE VANITY OF HUMAN WISHES.'

In this Satire JOHNSON followed the theme of the *Tenth* Satire of JUVENAL, the argument of which is given as it prefaces DRYDEN'S translation. The chief passages in JUVENAL with DRYDEN'S interpretation, from which JOHNSON evidently derived his inspiration, are appended to the text, though his illustrations are taken from modern history.

ARGUMENT OF THE TENTH SATIRE OF JUVENAL.

The poet's design in this Satire is to represent the various wishes and desires of mankind ; and to set out the folly of them. He runs through all the several heads of riches, honours, eloquence, fame for martial achieve-ments, long life, and beauty ; and gives instances, in each, how frequently they have proved the ruin of those that owned them. He concludes therefore, that since we generally choose so ill for ourselves, we should do better to leave it to the gods to make the choice for us. All we can safely ask of Heaven lies within a very small com-pass. It is but health of body and mind. And if we have these, it is not much matter what we want besides ; for we have enough already to make us happy.

LONDON.

A POEM, IN IMITATION OF THE THIRD SATIRE OF JUVENAL, WRITTEN IN 1738.

... Quis ineptæ
Tam patiens urbis, tam ferreus, ut teneat se ?—Juv.

The small numerals refer to the Notes.

THOUGH grief and fondness in my breast rebel,
When injured Thales[1] bids the town farewell;
Yet still my calmer thoughts his choice commend,
I praise the hermit, but regret the friend,
Who now resolves, from vice and London far,[2]   5
To breathe in distant fields a purer air;
And fix'd on Cambria's solitary shore,
Give to St. David one true Briton more.

    For who would leave, unbribed, Hibernia's land,
Or change the rocks of Scotland for the Strand?   10
There none are swept by sudden fate away,
But all, whom hunger spares, with age decay:

1-8. *Though grief* . . . .
. . . . . . *Briton more.*
Quamvis digressu veteris confusus amici,
Laudo tamen vacuis quod sedem figere Cumis
Destinet, atque unum civem donare Sybillæ.
                  JUVENAL, III., 1-3.

    Grieved though I am an ancient friend to lose,
    I like the solitary seat he chose;
    In quiet Cumæ fixing his repose.
    Where far from noisy Rome secure he lives,
    And one more citizen to Sibyl gives.—DRYDEN, 1-5.

Here malice, rapine, accident conspire,
† And now a rabble rages, now a fire ;
Their ambush here relentless ruffians lay,   15
And here the fell attorney prowls for prey ;
Here falling houses thunder on your head,
And here a female atheist talks you dead.

    While Thales waits the wherry that contains
Of dissipated wealth the small remains,   20
On Thames's banks, in silent thought we stood ;
Where Greenwich smiles upon the silver flood :
Struck with the seat that gave Eliza birth,[3]
We kneel, and kiss the consecrated earth ;
In pleasing dreams the blissful age renew,   25
And call Britannia's glories back to view ;

    13-18 *Here malice* .   .   .   .
.   .   .   .   .   .   *you dead.*
.   .   .   .   .   ut non
Deterius credas horrere incendia, lapsus
Tectorum assiduos, ac mille pericula sævæ
Urbis, et Augusto recitantes mense Poëtas.
                    JUVENAL, III., 6-9.
What scene so desert, or so full of fright,
As towering houses tumbling in the night,
And Rome on fire beheld by its own blazing light ?
But worse than all, the clattering tiles ; and worse
Than thousand padders is the poet's curse.
Rogues that in dog days cannot rhyme forbear,
But without mercy read, and make you hear.
                    DRYDEN, 10-16.

    19-21. *While Thales* .   .   .   .   .
.   .   .   .   .   .   *we stood.*
Sed dum tota domus rhedâ componitur unâ.
                    JUVENAL, III., 10.
Now while my friend, just ready to depart,
Was packing all his goods in one poor cart,
He stopped a little at the conduit gate.
                    DRYDEN, 17-19.

Behold her cross triumphant on the main,
The guard of commerce, and the dread of Spain,
Ere masquerades debauch'd, excise oppress'd,[5]
Or English honour grew a standing jest.   30
    A transient calm the happy scenes bestow,
And for a moment lull the sense of woe.
At length awaking, with contemptuous frown,
Indignant Thales eyes the neighb'ring town :
' Since worth,' he cries, ' in these degenerate days,   35
Wants e'en the cheap reward of empty praise ;
In those cursed walls, devote to vice and gain,
Since unrewarded science toils in vain ;
Since hope but soothes to double my distress,
And every moment leaves my little less ;   40
While yet my steady steps no staff sustains,
And life still vig'rous revels in my veins ;

31-34. *A transient* . . . . . .
     . . . . . *neighb'ring town.*

Hic tunc Umbritius.—JUVENAL, III., 21.

Into this lonely vale our steps we bend,
I and my sullen discontented friend.

  . . . .
Then thus Umbritius (with an angry frown),
And looking back on this degenerate town.
                  DRYDEN, 30-38.

41, 42. *While yet* . . . . . .
     . . . . *my veins.*

Dum nova canities, dum prima et recta senectus,
Dum superest Lachesi, quod torqueat et pedibus me
Porto meis, nullo dextram subeunte bacillo.
                JUVENAL, III., 26-29.

While yet few furrows on my face are seen,
While I walk upright, and old age is green.
                  DRYDEN, 43, 44.

Grant me, kind Heaven, to find some happier place,
Where honesty and sense are no disgrace ;
Some pleasing bank where verdant osiers play,   45
Some peaceful vale with Nature's paintings gay ;
Where once the harass'd Briton found repose,
And safe in poverty defied his foes ;
Some secret cell, ye powers indulgent, give,
Let —— live here, for —— has learn'd to live.   50
Here let those reign whom pensions can incite [6]
To vote a patriot black, a courtier white ;
Explain their country's dear-bought rights away,
And plead for pirates in the face of day ; [7]
With slavish tenets taint our poison'd youth,   55
And lend a lie the confidence of truth.
Let such raise palaces, and manors buy,
Collect a tax, or farm a lottery ; [8]
With warbling eunuchs fill our silenced stage,[9]
And lull to servitude a thoughtless age.   60

  ' Heroes, proceed ! what bounds your pride shall hold ?
What check restrain your thirst of power and gold ?
Behold rebellious Virtue quite o'erthrown,
Behold our fame, our wealth, our lives your own.

51-58. *Here let* . . . . *a lottery.*

. . . . maneant qui nigra in candida vertunt,
Queis facile est ædem conducere, flumina, portus,
Siccandam eluviem, portandum ad busta cadaver.
                          JUVENAL, III., 30-32.

Such manners will with such a town agree :
Knaves who in full assemblies have the knack
Of turning truth to lies, and white to black,
Can hire large houses, and oppress the poor
By *farmed excise* ; can cleanse the common sewer,
And rent the fishery ; can bear the dead,
And teach their eyes dissembled tears to shed,
All this for gain : for gain they sell their very head.
                          DRYDEN, 53-60.

To such the plunder of a land is given,   65
When public crimes inflame the wrath of Heaven :
But what, my friend, what hope remains for me,
Who start at theft, and blush at perjury ?
Who scarce forbear, though Britain's court he sing,
To pluck a titled poet's borrow'd wing ;   70
A statesman's logic unconvinced can hear,
And dare to slumber o'er the Gazetteer :
Despise a fool in half his pension dress'd,
And strive in vain to laugh at * H——y's jest.[10]
   ' Others, with softer smiles and subtler art   75
Can sap the principles, or taint the heart ;
With more address a lover's note convey,
Or bribe a virgin's innocence away.
Well may they rise, while I, whose rustic tongue
Ne'er knew to puzzle right, or varnish wrong,   80
Spurn'd as a beggar, dreaded as a spy,
Live unregarded, unlamented die.
   ' For what but social guilt the friend endears ?
Who shares Orgilio's [11] crimes, his fortunes shares.
But thou, should tempting villany present   85
All Marlborough[12] hoarded, or all Villiers[13] spent,
Turn from the glittering bribe thy scornful eye,
Nor sell for gold what gold could never buy,
The peaceful slumber, self-approving day,
Unsullied fame, and conscience ever gay.   90

67, 68. *But what* . . . . *at perjury?*
   Quid Romæ faciam? mentiri nescio : librum
   Si malus est nequeo laudare et poscere . . .
                              JUVENAL, III., 41, 42.
   What's Rome to me, what business have I there,
   I who can neither lie, nor falsely swear?
                              DRYDEN, 81, 82.

* In Sir JOHN HAWKINS's edition, 1787, this line is—
   And strive in vain to laugh at Clodio's jest.

In an earlier edition of 1785, corrected from a copy printed at the
Clarendon Press, Oxford, the line is as we have given it in the Text.

'The cheated nation's happy fav'rites, see !
Mark whom the great caress, who frown on me !
London ! the needy villain's general home,
The common sewer of Paris and of Rome,[14]
With eager thirst, by folly or by fate,   95
Sucks in the dregs of each corrupted state.
Forgive my transports on a theme like this,
I cannot bear a French metropolis.
   'Illustrious Edward ; [15] from the realms of day,
The land of heroes and of saints survey !   100
Nor hope the British lineaments to trace,
The rustic grandeur, or the surly grace ;
But, lost in thoughtless ease and empty show,
Behold the warrior dwindled to a beau ;
Sense, freedom, piety, refined away,   105
Of France the mimic, and of Spain the prey.
   'All that at home no more can beg or steal,

93-98. *London ! the* . . . . . .
         . . . . *French metropolis.*

. . . . . Non possum ferre, Quirites,
Græcam urbem . . .   JUVENAL, III., 60.

I hate in Rome a Grecian town to find,
To see the scum of Greece transplanted there.
                             DRYDEN, 106, 107.

107-112. *All that* . . . . . .
         . . . . *they prey.*

Jampridem Syrus in Tiberim defluxit Orontes,
Et linguam et mores et cum tibicine chordas
Obliquas, necnon gentilia tympana secum
Vexit, ...
                          JUVENAL, III., 62-65.

Conveys his wealth to Tyber's hungry shores,
And surfeits Italy with loose amours ;
Hither their crooked harps, and customs come,
All find receipt in hospitable Rome.
                          DRYDEN 111-114.

Or like a gibbet better than a wheel ; [16]
Hiss'd from the stage, or hooted from the court,
Their air, their dress, their politics import ;   110
Obsequious, artful, voluble, and gay,
On Britain's fond credulity they prey.
No gainful trade their industry can 'scape,
They sing, they sew, clean shoes, their fiddles scrape :
All sciences a fasting Monsieur knows, [17]   115
And bid him go to hell, to hell he goes.
    ' Ah ! what avails it that, from slavery far,
I draw the breath of life in English air ;
Was early taught a Briton's right to prize,
And lisp the tale of Henry's victories ; [18]   120
If the gull'd conqueror receives the chain,
And flattery subdues when arms are vain ?
    ' Studious to please, and ready to submit,
The supple Gaul was born a parasite :
Still to his interest true, where'er he goes,   125
Wit, bravery, worth, his lavish tongue bestows ;

113, 116. *All sciences*   .   .   .   .   .   .
       .   .   .   .   .   .   *he goes.*
                    Omnia novit
       Græculus esuriens, in cœlum jusseris, ibit.
                         JUVENAL, III., 77, 78.

       All things the hungry Greek exactly knows
       And bid him go to heaven, to heaven he goes.
                         DRYDEN, 113, 114.

123 124. *Studious to*   .   .   .   .   .   .
       .   .   .   .   .   .   *a parasite.*

       .   .   .   .   adulandi gens prudentissima, laudat
       Sermonem indocti, faciem deformis amici.
                         JUVENAL, III., 86, 87.

       The Greeks get all by fulsome flatteries,
       A most peculiar stroke they have at lies
                         DRYDEN, 151, 152.

In every face a thousand graces shine,
From every tongue flows harmony divine.
These arts in vain our rugged natives try,
Strain out with faltering diffidence a lie,
And gain a kick for awkward flattery.
    ' Besides, with justice, this discerning age
Admires their wondrous talents for the stage : [19]
Well may they venture on the mimic's art,
Who play from morn to night a borrow'd part :   135
Practised their master's notions to embrace,
Repeat his maxims, and reflect his face !
With every wild absurdity comply,
And view each object with another's eye ;
To shake with laughter ere the jest they hear,   140
To pour at will the counterfeited tear ;
And, as their patron hints the cold or heat,
To shake in dog-days, in December sweat.

130

140-143. *To shake* . . . .
        . . . . . *December sweat.*

Natio comœda est : rides : majore cachinno
Concutitur : flet : si lacrymas auspexit amici :
Nec dolet : igniculum brumæ si tempore poscas
Accipit endromidem : si dixeris, æstuo, sudat.
                                    JUVENAL, III., 100-104.

All Greece is one comedian : laugh and they
Return it louder than an ass can bray :
Grieve and they grieve ; if you weep silently,
There seems a silent echo in their eye.
They cannot mourn like you, but they can cry,
Call for a fire, their winter clothes they take.
Begin but you to shiver, and they shake.
In frost or snow, if you complain of heat
They rub th' unsweating brow and swear they sweat.
                                    DRYDEN, 170-180.

How, when competitors like these contend,
Can surly Virtue hope to fix a friend ?   145
Slaves that with serious impudence beguile,
And lie without a blush, without a smile ;
Exalt each trifle, every vice adore,
Your taste in snuff, your lewdness flatter more ;
Can Balbo's eloquence applaud, and swear   150
He gropes his breeches with a monarch's air !
    ' For arts like these preferr'd, admired, caress'd,
They first invade your table, then your breast ;
Explore your secrets with insidious art,
Watch the weak hour, and ransack all the heart ;   155
Then soon your ill-plac'd confidence repay,
Commence your lords, and govern or betray.
    ' By numbers here, from shame or censure free,
All crimes are safe but hated poverty :
This, only this, the rigid law pursues,   160
This, only this, provokes the snarling muse.

144, 145. *How when*   .   .   .   .
         .   .   .   . *a friend ?*

       Non sumus ergo pares : melior qui semper
       Nocte dieque alienum sumere vultum.
                JUVENAL, III., 104, 105.

       We are not on the square with such as these,
       Such are our betters who can better please.
                DRYDEN, 179, 180.

154-157 *Explore your*   .   .   '   .   .   .   .
         .   .   .   . *or betray.*

       Scire volunt secreta domus atque inde timeri.
                JUVENAL, III., 113.

       They search the secrets of the house, and so
       Are worshipped there and feared for what they know.
                DRYDEN, 194, 195.

The sober trader at a tatter'd cloak
Wakes from his dream, and labours for a joke ;
With brisker air the silken courtiers gaze,
And turn the varied taunt a thousand ways.   165
Of all the griefs that harass the distress'd,
Sure the most bitter is a scornful jest ; [20]
Fate never wounds more deep the generous heart
Than when a blockhead's insult points the dart.
    ' Has Heaven reserved, in pity to the poor,   170
No pathless waste, or undiscover'd shore ?
No secret island in the boundless main ?
No peaceful desert yet unclaim'd by Spain ? [21]
Quick let us rise, the happy seats explore,
And bear Oppression's insolence no more. [22]   175
This mournful truth is everywhere confess'd :
SLOW RISES WORTH, BY POVERTY DEPRESS'D :
But here more slow, where all are slaves to gold,
Where looks are merchandise, and smiles are sold ;

166, 167. _Of all_ . . . .
     . . . . . _scornful jest._

    Nil habet infelix paupertas durius in se
    Quam quod ridiculos homines facit.
                JUVENAL, III., 152, 153.

    Want is the scorn of every wealthy fool,
    And wit in rags is turned to ridicule.
                DRYDEN, 256, 257.

176, 177. _This mournful_ . . . . .
     . . . . . _poverty depress'd._

    Haud facile emergunt, quorum virtutibus obstat
    Res angusta domi . . . .
                JUVENAL, III., 164, 165.

    Rarely they rise by virtue's aid, who lie
    Plunged in the depth of helpless poverty.
                DRYDEN, 275, 276.

Where, won by bribes, by flatteries implor'd,   180
The groom retails the favours of his lord.
   ' But hark ! th' affrighted crowd's tumultuous cries
Roll through the streets, and thunder to the skies :
Raised from some pleasing dream of wealth and power,
Some pompous palace, or some blissful bower,   185
Aghast you start, and scarce with aching sight
Sustain the approaching fire's tremendous light ;
Swift from pursuing horrors take your way,
And leave your little ALL to flames a prey ;
Then through the world a wretched vagrant roam, 190
For where can starving Merit find a home ?
In vain your mournful narrative disclose,
While all neglect, and most insult your woes.
   ' Should Heaven's just bolts Orgilio's wealth con-
      found,
And spread his flaming palace on the ground,   195

186-189. *Aghast you* . . . . . .
    . . . . *a prey.*

     Vivendum est illic, ubi nulla incendia, nulli
     Nocte metus : jam poscit aquam, jam frivola transfert
     Ucalegon . . .   JUVENAL, III., 197-199.

     At Cumæ we can sleep, quite round the year,
     Nor falls, nor fires, nor nightly dangers fear,
     While rolling flames from Roman turrets fly
     And the pale citizens for buckets cry,
     Thy neighbour has removed his wretched store
     (Few hands will rid the lumber of the poor).
                DRYDEN, 321-325.

194-203. *Should heaven's* . . . . . .
    . . . . . . *rising dome.*

     Si magna Asturii cecidit domus : horrida mater,
     Pullati proceres, differt vadimonia prætor : ·
     Tunc gemimus casus urbis, tunc odimus ignem.

               D

Swift o'er the land the dismal rumour flies,
And public mournings pacify the skies ;
The laureate tribe in venal verse relate
How Virtue wars with persecuting Fate ;
With well-feign'd gratitude the pension'd band   200
Refund the plunder of the beggar'd land.
See ! while he builds, the gaudy vassals come,
And crowd with sudden wealth the rising dome;
The price of boroughs and of souls restore,
And raise his treasures higher than before :   205
Now bless'd with all the baubles of the great,
The polish'd marble, and the shining plate,
Orgilio sees the golden pile aspire,
And hopes from angry Heaven another fire.
    'Couldst thou resign the park and play content,210
For the fair banks of Severn or of Trent ;
There might'st thou find some elegant retreat,
Some hireling senator's deserted seat,
And stretch thy prospects o'er the smiling land,
For less than rent the dungeons of the Strand ;   215
There prune thy walks, support thy drooping flow'rs,
Direct thy rivulets, and twine thy bow'rs :
And while thy beds a cheap repast afford,
Despise the dainties of a venal lord :

> Ardet adhuc, et jam accurrit qui marmora donet,
> Conferat impensas   .   .   .   .   .
> > JUVENAL, III., 212-216.

> But if the palace of Arturius burn
> The nobles change their clothes, the matrons mourn ;
> The city Prætor will no pleadings hear,
> And look aghast as if the Gauls were here ;
> While yet it burns, th' officious nation flies
> Some to condole, and some to bring supplies ;
> One sends him marble to rebuild, and one
> White naked statues of the Parian stone.
> > DRYDEN, 345-353.

There every bush with nature's music rings, 220
There every breeze bears health upon its wings ;
On all thy hours security shall smile,————
And bless thine evening walk and morning toil)
   ' Prepare for death, if here at night you roam ;
And sign your will, before you sup from home. 225
Some fiery fop, with new commission vain,(23)

ˀee p. 62
for cond[...]
in[...]

224, 225. *Prepare for* . . . . . .
    . . . . . *from home.*
    . . . . Possis ignavus haberi,
Et subiti casus improvidus, ad cœnam si
Intestatus eas . . . .
              JUVENAL, III., 272-274.
'Tis want of sense to sup abroad too late,
Unless thou first hast settled thy estate.
              DRYDEN, 434, 435.

226-235. *Some fiery* . . . . . .
    . . . . . *golden coach.*
Ebrius, ac petulans, qui nullum forte cecidit,
Dat pœnas, noctem patitur lugentis amicum
Pelidæ . . . .
    . . . Sed quamvis improbus annis,
Atque mero fervens, cavet hunc, quem coccina læna
Vitari jubet, et comitum longissimus ordo :
Multum præterea flammarum, atque ænea lampas.
             JUVENAL, III., 278-285.
The scouring drunkard, if he does not fight
Before his bedtime, takes no rest that night,
Passing the tedious hours in greater pain
Than stern Achilles, when his friend was slain.

. . . .
Yet though his youthful blood be fired with wine,
He wants not wit the danger to decline ;
Is cautious to avoid the coach and six,
And on the lackeys will no quarrel fix :
His train of flambeaux, and embroidered coat,
May privilege my lord to walk on foot.
             DRYDEN, 440-450.

Who sleeps on brambles till he kills his man ;
Some frolic drunkard, reeling from a feast,
Provokes a broil, and stabs you for a jest.
   ' Yet e'en these heroes, mischievously gay,   230
Lords of the street, and terrors of the way ;
Flush'd as they are with folly, youth, and wine,
Their prudent insults to the poor confine ;
Afar they mark the flambeau's bright approach
And shun the shining train and golden coach.   235
   ' In vain, these dangers past, your doors you
     close,
And hope the balmy blessings of repose :
Cruel with guilt, and daring with despair,—
The midnight murd'rer bursts the faithless bar ;
Invades the sacred hour of silent rest,   240
And plants, unseen, a dagger in your breast.

236–241. *In vain* . . . .
. . . . *your breast.*

    Nec tamen hoc tantum metuas : nam qui spoliet te
    Non deerit : clausis domibus, postquam omnis ubique
    Fixa catenatæ siluit compago tabernæ.
    Interdum et ferro subitus grassator agit rem.
            JUVENAL, III., 302–305.

    Nor is this all : for when retired you think
    To sleep securely ; when the candles wink,
    When every door with iron chains is barred
    And roaring taverns are no longer heard,
    The ruffian robbers, by no justice awed,
    And unpaid cutthroat soldiers are abroad ;
    These venal souls, who, hardened in each ill,
    To save complaints and prosecution, kill.
            DRYDEN, 474–481.

'Scarce can our fields, such crowds at Tyburn die,[24]
With hemp the gallows and the fleet supply.
Propose your schemes, ye senatorian band,
Whose ways and means support the sinking land ; 245
Lest ropes be wanting in the tempting spring,
To rig another convoy for the king.[25]
    ' A single jail, in Alfred's golden reign,[26]
Could half the nation's criminals contain ;
Fair Justice then, without constraint ador'd,   250
Held high the steady scale, but sheath'd the sword ;
No spies were paid, no special juries known ;
Blest age ! but ah ! how diff'rent from our own !
    ' Much could I add,--but see the boat at hand,
The tide retiring, calls me from the land :   255

242, 243. *Scarce can*   .   .   .   .   .   .
    .   .   .   .   .   . *fleet supply.*
248, 249. *A single*   .   .   .   .   .   .
    .   .   .   .   . *criminals contain.*

Qua fornace graves, qua non incude catenæ ?
Maximus in vinclis ferri modus, ut timeas, ne
Vomer deficiat, ne marræ et sarcula desint.
Felices proavorum atavos, felicia dicas
Sæcula, quæ quondam sub regibus atque tribunis
Viderunt uno contentam carcere Romam.
                     JUVENAL, III., 309-314.

The forge in fetters only is employed,
Our iron mines exhausted and destroyed
In shackles : for these villains scarce allow
Goads for the teams, and ploughshares for the plough.
Oh happy ages of our ancestors !
Beneath the kings and tribunitial powers
One jail did all their criminals restrain,
Which, now, the walls of Rome can scarce contain.
                     DRYDEN, 486-492.

Farewell !—When youth, and health, and fortune spent,
Thou fliest for refuge to the wilds of Kent ;
And, tired like me with follies and with crimes,
In angry numbers warn'st succeeding times ;
Then shall thy friend, nor thou refuse his aid,   260
Still foe to vice, forsake his Cambrian shade ;
In Virtue's cause once more exert his rage,
Thy satire point, and animate thy page.'

THE

VANITY OF HUMAN WISHES.

IN IMITATION OF THE TENTH SATIRE OF JUVENAL.

LET observation, with extensive view,
Survey mankind from China to Peru;
Remark each anxious toil, each eager strife,
And watch the busy scenes of crowded life ;
Then say how hope and fear, desire and hate, 5
O'erspread with snares the clouded maze of fate,[1]
Where wav'ring man betray'd by vent'rous pride,
To chase the dreary paths, without a guide,
As treach'rous phantoms in the mist delude,
Shuns fancied ills, or chases airy good ; 10
How rarely reason guides the stubborn choice,
Rules the bold hand, or prompts the suppliant voice ;
How nations sink by darling schemes oppress'd,*
When vengeance listens to the fool's request.
Fate wings with ev'ry wish th' afflictive dart, 15
Each gift of nature and each grace of art :
With fatal heat impetuous courage glows,
With fatal sweetness elocution flows,

17, 18. *With fatal   .   .   . elocution flows.*

.   .   .   . Nocitura togâ, nocitura petuntur
Militiâ. Torrens dicendi copia multis,
Et sua mortifera est facundia. .   .   .   .   .
                                    JUVENAL, X., 8–10.

With laurels some have fatally been crowned ;
Some, who the depths of eloquence have found
In that unnavigable stream were drowned.
                                    DRYDEN, 11–13.

---

* This alludes to the financial troubles arising from the South
Sea Bubble and French Mississippi Scheme. (See note 3, line 34.)

Impeachment stops the speaker's powerful breath,[2]
And restless fire precipitates on death.   20
. But, scarce observed, the knowing and the bold,
Fall in the general massacre of gold ;
Wide wasting pest ! that rages unconfined,
And crowds with crimes the records of mankind ;
For gold his sword the hireling ruffian draws,   25
For gold the hireling judge distorts the laws ;
Wealth heap'd on wealth, nor truth nor safety buys,
The dangers gather as the treasures rise.
     Let history tell where rival kings command,
And dubious title shakes the madded land,   30
When statutes glean the refuse of the sword,
How much more safe the vassal than the lord;
Low skulks the hind beneath the rage of pow'r,
And leaves the wealthy traitor in the Tow'r,[3]

21, 23. *But, scarce*   .   .   .   .   .   .
     .   .   . *wasting pest !*
Sed plures nimiâ congesta pecunia curâ
Strangulat . . .   JUVENAL, X., 12, 13.

But more have been by avarice opprest,
And heaps of money crowded in the chest.
                              DRYDEN, 16, 17.

31–36. *When statutes*   .   .   .   .   .   .
     .   .   .   .   .   *hover round.*
Temporibus diris igitur, jussuque Neronis
Longinum, et magnos Senecæ prædivitis hortos
Clausit, et egregias Lateranorum obsidet ædes
Tota cohors : rarus venit in cœnacula miles.
                           JUVENAL, X., 15-18

For this in Nero's arbitrary time
When virtue was a guilt, and wealth a crime.
A troop of cutthroat guards were sent to seize
The rich men's goods, and gut their palaces ;
The mob commissioned by the government
Are seldom to an empty garret sent.—DRYDEN, 23-28.

Untouch'd his cottage, and his slumbers sound, . 35
Tho' confiscation's vultures hover round.

The needy traveller,[4] serene and gay,
Walks the wild heath and sings his toil away   *wealth*
Does envy seize thee? crush th' upbraiding joy,
Increase his riches, and his peace destroy.   40
Now fears in dire vicissitude invade,
The rustling brake alarms, and quiv'ring shade,
Nor light nor darkness bring his pain relief,
One shows the plunder, and one hides the thief.

Yet still one gen'ral cry the skies assails,   45
And gain and grandeur load the tainted gales;
Few know the toiling statesman's fear or care,   *Fred. Prince of*
Th' insidious rival and the gaping heir.[5]   *Wales.*

Once more, Democritus,[6] arise on earth,
With cheerful wisdom and instructive mirth,   50
See motley life in modern trappings dress'd,
And feed with varied fools th' eternal jest:
Thou who couldst laugh, where want enchain'd
          caprice,
Toil crush'd conceit, and man was of a piece;   55
Where wealth unloved without a mourner died;
And scarce a sycophant was fed by pride?

37–38. *The needy* . . . . . .
          . . . . . *toil away.*
Cantabit vacuus coram latrone viator.—JUVENAL, x., 22.

The beggar sings, e'en when he sees the place
Beset with thieves, and never mends his pace.
          DRYDEN, 33, 34.

45, 46. *Yet still* . . . .
          . . . . . *tainted gales.*
Prima fere vota, et cunctis notissima templis,
Divitiæ ut crescant, ut opes.—JUVENAL, X. 23, 24.

Of all the vows the first and chief request
Of each is, to be richer than the rest.—DRYDEN, 35, 36.

Where ne'er was known the form of mock debate,
Or seen a new-made mayor's unwieldy state ; [7]
Where change of fav'rites made no change of laws,   60
And senates heard before they judg'd a cause ;
How wouldst thou shake at Britain's modish tribe,
Dart the quick taunt, and edge the piercing gibe ?
Attentive truth and nature to descry,
And pierce each scene with philosophic eye.   65
To thee were solemn toys, or empty show,
The robes of pleasure, and the veils of woe :
All aid the farce, and all thy mirth maintain,
Whose joys are causeless, or whose griefs are vain.

Such was the scorn that fill'd the sage's mind,   70
Renew'd at ev'ry glance on human kind ;
How just that scorn ere yet thy voice declare,
Search ev'ry state, and canvass ev'ry prayer.
Unnumber'd suppliants crowd Preferment's gate,
Athirst for wealth, and burning to be great ;   75
Delusive Fortune hears th' incessant call,
They mount, they shine, evaporate, and fall.
On ev'ry stage the foes of peace attend,
Hate dogs their flight, and insult mocks their end.
Love ends with hope, the sinking statesman's door* 80
Pours in the morning worshipper no more ;
For growing names the weekly scribbler lies,

74–77. *Unnumbered suppliants* . . . *and fall.*
Quosdam præcipitat subjecta potentia magnæ
Invidiæ : mergit longa atque insignis honorum
Pagina ; descendunt statuæ restemque sequuntur.
JUVENAL, X., 56–58.
Some ask for envied power ; which public hate
Pursues, and hurries headlong to their fate.
Down go the titles ; and the statue crowned
Is by base hands in the next river drowned.
DRYDEN, 85–88.

* Alluding to the fall of Sir R. WALPOLE, 1742.

To growing wealth the dedicator flies ;
From ev'ry room descends the painted face,
That hung the bright palladium of the place ;[8]   85
And, smoked in kitchens, or in auctions sold,
To better features yields the frame of gold ;
For now no more we trace in ev'ry line
Heroic worth, benevolence divine :
The form distorted justifies the fall,   90
And detestation rids th' indignant wall.
    But will not Britain hear the last appeal[9]
Sign her foe's doom, or guard her fav'rite's zeal?
Through Freedom's sons no more remonstrance rings,
Degrading nobles, and controlling kings [10]:   95
Our supple tribes * repress their patriot throats,
And ask no questions but the price of votes ;
With weekly libels and septennial ale,[11]
Their wish is full to riot and to rail.
    In full-blown dignity, see Wolsey stand,[12]   100
Law in his voice, and fortune in his hand :
To him the church, the realm, their powers consign,
Through him the rays of regal bounty shine,
Turn'd by his nod the stream of honour flows,
His smile alone security bestows :   105
Still to new heights his restless wishes tow'r,
Claim leads to claim, and pow'r advances pow'r :
Till conquest unresisted ceas'd to please,
And rights submitted left him none to seize :
At length his sov'reign frowns [13]—the train of state 110
Mark the keen glance, and watch the sign to hate.
Where'er he turns, he meets a stranger's eye,
His suppliants scorn him, and his followers fly ;
Now drops at once the pride of awful state,
The golden canopy, the glitt'ring plate,   115
The regal palace, the luxurious board,
The liv'ried army, and the menial lord.

* i.e. constituencies.

With age, with cares, with maladies oppress'd,
He seeks the refuge of monastic rest.
Grief aids disease, remember'd folly stings,   120
And his last sighs reproach the faith of kings.
    Speak thou whose thoughts at humble peace repine,
Shall Wolsey's wealth with Wolsey's end be thine?
Or livest thou now, with safer pride content,
The wisest justice on the banks of Trent?   125
For, why did Wolsey, near the steeps of fate,
On weak foundations raise the enormous weight? ·
Why, but to sink beneath misfortune's blow,
With louder ruin to the gulfs below?
    What gave great Villiers to the assassin's knife,[14] 130
And fixed disease on Harley's closing life [15]?
What murdered Wentworth,[16] and what exiled Hyde,[17]
By kings protected, and to kings allied?
What but their wish indulged in courts to shine,
And pow'r too great to keep or to resign?   135
    When first the college rolls receive his name,
The young enthusiast quits his ease for fame ;
Resistless burns the fever of renown,
Caught from the strong contagion of the gown :
O'er Bodley's dome [18] his future labours spread,   140
And Bacon's mansion trembles o'er his head.[19]

136–141. *When first* . . . . . .
   . . . . *his head.*

    Eloquium ac famam Demosthenis, aut Ciceronis
    Incipit optare, et totis Quinquatribus optat,
    Quisquis adhuc uno partam colit asse Minervam,
    Quem sequitur custos angustæ vernula capsæ.
              JUVENAL, X., 114–117.

    The boy who scarce has paid his entrance down
    To his proud pedant, or declined a noun,
    So small an elf, that when the days are foul,
    He and his satchel must be borne to school,
    Yet prays and hopes, and aims at nothing less,
    To prove a Tully or Demosthenes.—DRYDEN, 180–185.

Are these thy views?   Proceed, illustrious youth,
And Virtue guard thee to the throne of Truth !
Yet should thy soul indulge the gen'rous heat
Till captive Science yields her last retreat;   145
Should Reason guide thee with her brightest ray,
And pour on misty Doubt resistless day ;
Should no false kindness lure to loose delight,
Nor praise relax, nor difficulty fright;
Should tempting Novelty thy cell refrain,   150
And Sloth effuse her opiate fumes in vain ;
Should Beauty blunt on fops her fatal dart,
Nor claim the triumph of a letter'd heart ;
Should no disease thy torpid veins invade,
Nor Melancholy's phantoms haunt thy shade ;   155
Yet hope not life from grief or danger free,
Nor think the doom of man revers'd for thee :
Deign on the passing world to turn thine eyes,
And pause awhile from letters to be wise ;
There mark what ills the scholar's life assail,   160
Toil, envy, want, the patron,* and the jail
See nations, slowly wise and meanly just,
To buried merit raise the tardy bust.[20]
If dreams yet flatter, once again attend,
Hear Lydiat's [21] life, and Galileo's end.[22]   165
  Nor deem, when Learning her last prize bestows,
The glitt'ring eminence exempt from foes ;
See, when the vulgar 'scapes, despised or awed,
Rebellion's vengeful talons seize on Laud.[23]
From meaner minds tho' smaller fines content,   170
The plunder'd palace,[24] or sequester'd rent,[25]
Mark'd out by dangerous parts, he meets the shock,
And fatal Learning leads him to the block :
Around his tomb let Art and Genius weep,
But hear his death, ye blockheads, hear and sleep. 175

* See Note A, p. 54.

The festal blazes, the triumphal show,
The ravish'd standard, and the captive foe,
The senate's thanks, the Gazette's pompous tale,[26]
With force resistless o'er the brave prevail.
Such bribes the rapid Greek o'er Asia whirl'd,   180
For such the steady Romans shook the world ;
For such in distant lands the Britons shine,
And stain with blood the Danube or the Rhine ; [27]
This power has praise, that virtue scarce can warm
Till fame supplies the universal charm.   185
Yet reason frowns on war's unequal game,
Where wasted nations raise a single name ;
And mortgaged states their grandsires' wreaths regret,
From age to age in everlasting debt ; [28]
Wreaths which at last the dear-bought right convey 190
To rust on medals, or on stones decay.
  On what foundation stands the warrior's pride,
How just his hopes, let Swedish Charles decide ; [29]
A frame of adamant, a soul of fire,
No dangers fright him, and no labours tire ;   195
O'er love, o'er fear, extends his wide domain,
Unconquer'd lord of pleasure and of pain ;
No joys to him pacific sceptres yield,
War sounds the trump, he rushes to the field ;
Behold surrounding kings their powers combine,[30] 200
And one capitulate,[31] and one resign ; [32]
Peace courts his hand, but spreads her charms in vain ;

203-205. *Think nothing* . . . . .
. . . . *polar sky.*

Actum, inquit, nihil est, nisi Pœno milite portas
Frangimus, et mediâ vexillum pono Suburrâ.
                JUVENAL, X., 155, 156.

Yet still uneasy cries— There's nothing done
Till level with the ground their gates are laid,
And Punic flags on Roman towers displayed.
                DRYDEN, 249-251.

'Think nothing gain'd,' he cries, 'till nought remain,
On Moscow's walls till Gothic standards fly,
And all be mine beneath the polar sky.'   205
The march begins in military state,
And nations on his eye suspended wait;
Stern Famine guards the solitary coast,
And Winter barricades the realms of Frost ;
He comes, nor want nor cold his course delay ;— 210
Hide, blushing glory, hide Pultowa's day ;[33]
The vanquish'd hero leaves his broken bands,
And shows his miseries in distant lands ;
Condemn'd a needy supplicant to wait,
While ladies interpose, and slaves debate.   215
But did not chance at length her error mend ?
Did no subverted empire mark his end ?
Did rival monarchs give the fatal wound ?
Or hostile millions press him to the ground ?
His fall was destin'd to a barren strand,   220
A petty fortress, and a dubious hand ;[34]
He left the name, at which the world grew pale,
To point a moral, or adorn a tale.
     All times their scenes of pompous woes afford,
From Persia's tyrant to Bavaria's lord.[35]   225
In gay hostility and barb'rous pride,
With half mankind embattled at his side,
Great Xerxes comes to seize the certain prey,
And starves exhausted regions in his way ;
Attendant Flatt'ry counts his myriads o'er,   230
Till counted myriads soothe his pride no more ;
Fresh praise is tried till madness fires his mind,
The waves he lashes, and enchains the wind ;

233. *The* . . . . . . *wind.*
   In Corum atque Eurum solitus sævire flagellis.
                              JUVENAL, 180.
   Who whipt the winds and made the sea his slave?
                              DRYDEN, 290.

New powers are claim'd, new powers are still bestow'd,
Till rude resistance lops the spreading god ;   235
The daring Greeks deride the martial show,
And heap their valleys with the gaudy foe ;
Th' insulted sea with humbler thought he gains,
A single skiff to speed his flight remains ;
Th' encumber'd oar scarce leaves the dreaded coast 240
Through purple billows and a floating host.
   The bold Bavarian, in a luckless hour,[36]   *Imp*
Tries the dread summits of Cæsarean power,[37]
With unexpected legions bursts away,
And sees defenceless realms receive his sway ;   245
Short sway : fair Austria spreads her mournful
     charms,[38]   *maria ther*
The queen, the beauty, sets the world in arms ;
From hill to hill the beacon's rousing blaze
Spreads wide the hope of plunder and of praise
The fierce Croatian, and the wild Hussar,[39]   250
With all the sons of ravage, crowd the war :
The baffled prince, in honour's flatt'ring bloom [40]
Of hasty greatness, finds the fatal doom ;
His foes' derision and his subjects' blame,
And steals to death from anguish and from shame. 255
   ' Enlarge my life with multitude of days ! '

256–259. *Enlarge my*   .   .   .   .   .   .   ,
     .   .   .   .   .   *protracted woe.*

     Da spatium vitæ, multos da, Jupiter annos
     Hoc recto vultu, solum hoc et pallidus optas,
     Sed quam continuis et quantis longa senectus
     Plena malis ! deformem et tetrum ante omnia vultum,
     Dissimilemque sui deformem pro cute pellem,
     Pendentesque genas, et tales aspice rugas.
                  JUVENAL, X., 188-193.

     Jove grant me length of life, and years good store
     Heap on my bending back, I ask no more.

In health, in sickness, thus the suppliant prays :
Hides from himself his state, and shuns to know,
That life protracted is protracted woe.
Time hovers o'er, impatient to destroy,   260
And shuts up all the passages of joy :
In vain their gifts the bounteous seasons pour,
The fruit autumnal, and the vernal flower ;
With listless eyes the dotard views the store,
He views, and wonders that they please no more ; 265
Now pall the tasteless meats, and joyless wines,
And Luxury with sighs her slave resigns.
Approach, ye minstrels, try the soothing strain,
Diffuse the tuneful lenitives of pain :
No sounds, alas ! would touch th' impervious ear, 270
Though dancing mountains witness'd Orpheus near ;
Nor lute nor lyre his feeble pow'rs attend,
Nor sweeter music of a virtuous friend ;
But everlasting dictates crowd his tongue,
Perversely grave, or positively wrong.   275
The still returning tale, and ling'ring jest,
Perplex the fawning niece and pamper'd guest,
While growing hopes scarce awe the gath'ring sneer,
And scarce a legacy can bribe to hear :
The watchful guests still hint the last offence ;   280
The daughter's petulance, the son's expense,
Improve his heady rage with treach'rous skill,
And mould his passions till they make his will.
    Unnumber'd maladies his joints invade,

> Both sick and healthful, old and young, conspire
> In this one silly mischievous desire ;
> Mistaken blessing, which old age they call,
> 'Tis a long nasty darksome hospital ;
> A ropy chain of rheums : a visage rough,
> Deformed, unfeatured, and a skin of buff.
>   DRYDEN, 301-308,

Lay siege to life, and press the dire blockade ; 285
But unextinguish'd av'rice still remains,
And dreaded losses aggravate his pains ;
He turns, with anxious heart and crippled hands,
His bonds of debt, and mortgages of lands ;
Or views his coffers with suspicious eyes, 290
Unlocks his gold, and counts it till he dies.
   But grant, the virtues of a temp'rate prime,
Bless with an age exempt from scorn or crime ;
An age that melts with unperceived decay,
And glides in modest innocence away ; 295
Whose peaceful day benevolence endears,
Whose night congratulating conscience cheers ;
The gen'ral fav'rite as the gen'ral friend :
Such age there is, and who shall wish its end ?
   Yet ev'n on this her load Misfortune flings, 300
To press the weary minutes' flagging wings ;
New sorrow rises as the day returns,
A sister sickens, or a daughter mourns.
Now kindred Merit fills the sable bier,
Now lacerated Friendship claims a tear ; 305
Year chases year, decay pursues decay,
Still drops some joy from with'ring life away ;
New forms arise, and diff'rent views engage,
Superfluous lags the vet'ran on the stage,
Till pitying Nature signs the last release, 310
And bids afflicted worth retire to peace.
   But few there are whom hours like these await, .
Who set unclouded in the gulfs of Fate.
From Lydia's monarch should the search descend,

314, 315. *From Lydia's* . . . .
. . . . *his end.*
   Et Crœsu·n, quem vox justi facunda Solonis
   Respicere ad longæ jussit spatia ultima vitæ.
                              JUVENAL, X., 274, 275.

By Solon caution'd to regard his end,   315
In life's last scene what prodigies surprise,
Fears of the brave, and follies of the wise ?
From Marlb'rough's eyes the streams of dotage flow,[41]
And Swift expires a driv'ler and a show.[42]
    The teeming mother, anxious for her race,   320
Begs for each birth the fortune of a face ;
Yet Vane could tell what ills from beauty spring ; [43]
And Sedley cursed the form that pleased a king.[44]
Ye nymphs of rosy lips and radiant eyes,
Whom pleasure keeps too busy to be wise ;   325
Whom joys with soft varieties invite,
By day the frolic, and the dance by night ;
Who frown with vanity, who smile with art,
And ask the latest fashion of the heart ;
What care, what rules, your heedless charms shall
    save,   330
Each nymph your rival, and each youth your slave ?

   . . . .   And rich Crœsus' fate
  Whom Solon wisely counselled to attend
  The name of happy, till he knew his end.
                DRYDEN, 421-423.

318, 319. *From Marlb'rough's*   . . . . .
  . . . . . . *a show.*

  Perdidit ille oculos, et luscis invidet : hujus
  Pallida labra cibum capiunt digitis alienis.
  . . . . . . sed omni,
  Membrorum damno major dementia, quæ vel
  Nomina servorum, nec vultum agnoscit amici.
            JUVENAL, X., 229-232.

  Another is of both his eyes bereft,
  And envies who has one for aiming left.

  . . . .

  His loss of members is a heavy curse,
  But all his faculties decayed—a worse.
            DRYDEN, 369-370.

Against your fame with fondness hate combines,
The rival batters, and the lover mines.
With distant voice neglected Virtue calls,
Less heard and less, the faint remonstrance falls ;   335
Tired with contempt, she quits the slipp'ry reign,
And Pride and Prudence take her seat in vain.
In crowd at once, where none the pass defend,
The harmless freedom, and the private friend.
The guardians yield, by force superior plied :   340
To Int'rest, Prudence ; and to Flatt'ry, Pride.
Here beauty falls, betray'd, despis'd, distress'd,
And hissing Infamy proclaims the rest.
    Where then shall Hope and Fear their objects find?
Must dull suspense corrupt the stagnant mind ?   345
Must helpless man, in ignorance sedate,
Roll darkling down the torrent of his fate ?
Must no dislike alarm, no wishes rise,
No cries invoke the mercies of the skies ?
Inquirer, cease ; petitions yet remain   350
Which Heav'n may hear, nor deem religion vain.
Still raise for good the supplicating voice,
But leave to Heav'n the measure and the choice :

344-353. *Where then*   .   .   .   .   .   .
    .   .   .   .   *the choice.*

Nil ergo optabunt hommes ? Si consilium vis,
Permittes ipsis expendere Numinibus, quid
Conveniat nobis, rebusque sit utile nostris.
                    JUVENAL, X., 346-349.

What then remains ? are we deprived of will ?
Must we not wish, for fear of wishing ill ?
Receive my counsel, and scarcely move,
Intrust thy fortune to the Powers above,
Leave them to manage for thee, and to grant
What their unerring wisdom sees thee want.
                    DRYDEN, 533-538.

Safe in his pow'r, whose eyes discern afar
The secret ambush of a specious pray'r !   355
Implore his aid, in his decisions rest,
Secure, whate'er he gives, he gives the best.
Yet, when the sense of sacred presence fires,
And strong devotion to the skies aspires,
Pour forth thy fervours for a healthful mind,   360
Obedient passions, and a will resign'd ;
For love, which scarce collective man can fill ;
For patience, sov'reign o'er transmuted ill ;
For faith, that, panting for a happier seat,
Counts death kind Nature's signal of retreat :   365
These goods for man the laws of Heav'n ordain,
These goods he grants, who grants the pow'r to gain ;
With these celestial Wisdom calms the mind,
And makes the happiness she does not find.

359–361. *Pour forth* . . . . . .
. . . . . . *will resigned.*

  Orandum est, ut sit mens sana in corpore sano.
        JUVENAL, X., 356.

. . . . . And stand confined
To health of body, and content of mind.
        DRYDEN, 548, 549.

  368. *With* . . . . . *mind.*

  Tranquillæ per virtutem patet unica vitæ.
        JUVENAL, X., 364.

  The path to peace is virtue.—DRYDEN, 558.

NOTE A. PAGE 45.

'*Toil, envy, want, the patron and the jail.*']   In the first edition of the 'Vanity of Human Wishes,' which was published in 1749, the word 'garret' was used instead of '*patron.*'   .

'Toil, envy, want, the *garret* and the jail.'

The disappointment and mortification JOHNSON underwent from the fallacious patronage of Lord CHESTERFIELD led to the change in the subsequent editions of garret for patron. 'Such treatment I did not expect, for I never had a patron before. . . . Is not a patron, my lord, one who looks with unconcern on a man struggling for life in the water, and when he has reached ground, encumbers him with help?' (JOHNSON'S Letter to Lord CHESTERFIELD, February 7, 1755.)   When this was written, private patronage had ceased to be munificent or encouraging, and public patronage —that of general readers and buyers—had not begun to be remunerative. (Vid. *Quar. Rev.*, April 1878.)

NOTES.

HISTORICAL AND BIOGRAPHICAL ALLUSIONS.

'*LONDON*.'

[1] *When injured Thales bids the town farewell.*] Sir JOHN HAWKINS tells us, ' The event is antedated in the poem of *London* ; but in every particular, except the difference of a year, what is there said of the departure of Thales must be understood of SAVAGE, and looked upon as *true history*.' This conjecture is, I believe, entirely groundless. I have been assured that JOHNSON said he was not so much as acquainted with SAVAGE when he wrote his *London*. If the departure mentioned in it was the departure of SAVAGE, the event was not antedated, but foreseen : for *London* was published in May 1738, and SAVAGE did not set out for Wales till July 1739. However well JOHNSON could defend the credibility of second sight, he did not pretend that he himself was possessed of that faculty. (BOSWELL'S *Life of Johnson*, ch. iii.)

The assertion that JOHNSON was not even acquainted with SAVAGE when he published his *London* may be doubtful. JOHNSON took leave of SAVAGE when he went to Wales in 1739, and must have been acquainted with him before that period. (A. CHALMERS.)

RICHARD SAVAGE (1696-1743), whose life JOHNSON wrote, was the bastard child of RICHARD SAVAGE, Earl Rivers, and the Countess of Macclesfield. He led a dissipated and erratic life, the victim of circumstances and his own passions. In his miscellaneous poems, the best are the *Wanderer* and the *Bastard*.[1]

---

[1] The most remarkable of the persons with whom at this time JOHNSON consorted was RICHARD SAVAGE, an earl's son, a shoemaker's apprentice, who had seen life in all its forms—who had feasted among blue ribands in St. James' Square, and had lain with fifty pounds' weight of irons on his legs in the condemned ward of Newgate. This man had, after many vicissitudes of fortune, sunk at last into abject and hopeless poverty. His pen had failed him ; his patrons had been taken away by death, or estranged by the riotous profusion with which he squandered their bounty and the ungrateful insolence with which he rejected their advice. He now lived by begging. He dined on venison and champagne whenever he had been so

¹²⁻² *From vice and London far.*] This contrast of the vice of towns with the innocence of country life was a favourite theme of poets in this century.

³ *Gave Eliza birth.*] Queen ELIZABETH was born at Greenwich, September 7, 1533.

⁴ *The guard of commerce and the dread of Spain.*] During the thirty years previous we had been involved in the following wars with Spain. From 1718–1720, and again from 1725–1727. The chief event in the former was the English naval victory off Cape Passaro (1718), and in the latter the siege of Gibraltar,¹ when the English were again victorious. At this time we were on the eve of a third war, in which ANSON distinguished himself.

⁵ *Excise oppress'd.*] The idea of excise at this period was strangely hateful to the people generally, In 1733 WALPOLE had laid before the House of Commons his great *Excise scheme.* He proposed a system of bonded warehousing, making London a port, free from customs. In vain did he show that, were the duties collected in the manner proposed, the amount produced would be so much larger than under the old system, that he would be able to remit other taxes. The national feeling was opposed to him, and though he passed the bill through the Commons by a majority of 61, he gave way amidst popular rejoicing. Cockades bearing the device *Liberty, Property,* and no *Excise,* were worn, and WALPOLE was burnt in effigy. He was, however, supported by the King, and his retirement from office, ardently expected, did not take place.

fortunate as to borrow a guinea. If his questing had been unsuccessful, he appeased the rage of hunger with some scraps of broken meat and lay down to rest under the Piazza of Covent Garden in warm weather, and in cold weather, as near as he could get to the furnace of a glasshouse. Yet, in his misery he was still an agreeable companion. He had an inexhaustible store of anecdotes about that gay and brilliant world from which he was now an outcast. He had observed the great men of both parties in hours of careless relaxation, had seen the leaders of opposition without the mask of patriotism, and had heard the prime minister roar with laughter and tell stories not over decent. During some months SAVAGE lived in the closest familiarity with JOHNSON, and then the friends parted not without tears. JOHNSON remained in London to drudge for CAVE ; SAVAGE went to the west of England, lived there as he had lived everywhere, and in 1743 died penniless and heartbroken in Bristol gaol. (*Encycl. Britannica.* Samuel Johnson, by Lord Macaulay.)

¹ Ceded to Great Britain by the Treaty of Utrecht 1713. The Spaniards made an abortive attempt to recapture it 1720. Again they besieged it from January to June 1727, when they were forced to retire.

[6] *Whom pensions can incite.*] From the period of the Restoration the House of Commons had contained a large portion of venality within its walls, though the phases of it were various. Direct bribes in hard cash were the first and simplest course, and this continued long to prevail. *Pensions*, which are of a similar nature, gradually came into operation. This phase means places for self, family and friends. It was against the system of pensions that the Opposition (1730) directed its efforts. There were already Acts incapacitating the holders of them sitting in the House of Commons; but they had proved useless, as Government would not tell who had pensions, and the amount of secret service money was considerable. Mr. SANDYS therefore brought in a Bill (1730) by which every member was to swear that he did not hold a pension, and that in case of his accepting one, he would make it known within fourteen days. This the king called a 'villanous Bill,' but WALPOLE would not incur the odium of opposing it, and it passed the Commons by a majority of 10, but was thrown out by the Lords, and its fate was similar whenever it was brought in again. In 1734, when Parliament was dissolved, bribery and corruption ran high. At the ensuing elections WALPOLE spent 60,000*l.* from his own private purse to influence the elections. In 1742 a Committee of Secresy was appointed to investigate the events of the last ten years of WALPOLE's administration. Though the witnesses were protected by a Bill of Indemnity, they refused to explain the use WALPOLE had made of secret service money, and the prosecution fell through.

[7] *And plead for pirates in the face of day.*] For many years the merchants had been making complaints of the injuries done to our West Indian trade by the right of search exercised by the Spanish *Guarda-costas*, or guard-ships, and the cruel treatment experienced by our sailors. 'The fable of Jenkins's ears,' as BURKE calls it, was of great service. This was a Scottish master of a ship, who said that seven years before he had been taken by a Spaniard who, besides treating him with great cruelty in other respects, cut off one of his ears, and bid him carry it to his king, whom he would serve in the same way if he were there. 'I then,' said JENKINS, 'recommended my soul to God and my cause to my country.' The story produced such an effect that PULTENEY declared that the very name of JENKINS would raise volunteers. JENKINS always carried the ear about him wrapped in cotton. Some said he had lost it in the pillory. The Opposition, glad to embarrass the Ministers, joined heartily in the cry. *Various attempts were made by* WALPOLE *to settle the matter by negotiation.* At length, rather than part with his power,

he yielded to the public will, contrary to his better judgment. War was therefore declared against Spain. THOMSON'S poem of *Britannia* will show how noble and generous minds were deceived at this time.

[8] *Farm a lottery.*] Lotteries originated among ourselves during the reign of Queen Elizabeth. The rage for speculation which characterised the people of England during the early part of the last century, which culminated in the South Sea Bubble, was favourable to all kinds of lottery speculation. Guildhall was a scene of great excitement during the drawing of prizes there, and poor medical students used to attend to blood in case the sudden proclaiming of the fate of tickets had an overwhelming effect. Westminster Bridge was built by lottery consisting of 125,000 tickets at 5*l.* each. In 1774 the brothers ADAM of the Adelphi Terrace, and the adjoining streets of the Strand, disposed of these by a lottery containing 110 prizes. At the close of last century lotteries had become established by successive Acts of Parliament, being considered as a means for increasing the revenue by our Chancellors of the Exchequer. Their abolition deprived the Government of a revenue of 250,000*l.* to 300,000*l.* per annum. On October 18, 1826, the last State lottery was drawn in England. (CHAMBERS'S *Book of Days*, ii. 465.)

[9] *A silenced stage.* Another reading is *licensed stage*, which is less forcible.] At the early part of the century scurrilous personalities, low buffoonery, and undisguised sedition took possession of the stage, and the licentiousness of morals under Charles II. was now exchanged for the licentiousness of liberty. The necessity to curb these excesses became evident to all parties. In 1737 an occasion offered for WALPOLE to effect his object. A farce called the *Golden Rump*, abounding in sedition and blasphemy, was brought to him in manuscript with the hope that he might give a considerable sum to purchase and suppress it. WALPOLE paid the money, and showed the objectionable passages to several members of both parties. Being promised their support, he brought in his famous *Playhouse Bill*, under the form of an amendment to the Vagrant Act. It declared that every actor without a legal settlement, or a license from the Lord Chamberlain, should be deemed a rogue and a vagabond. To the Lord Chamberlain it gave legal power instead of customary privilege; authorising him to prohibit the representation of any drama at his discretion, and compelling all authors to send copies of their plays fourteen days before they were acted, under forfeiture of 50*l.* and of the license of the house.

Lord CHESTERFIELD, in opposing it in the Lords, admitted
that he had observed of late a remarkable licentiousness in the stage.
In one play very lately acted, *Pasquin* (by FIELDING) the author
thought fit to represent the three great professions, Religion, Physic,
and Law, as inconsistent with common sense ; in another (*King
Charles the First*) a most tragic story, was brought upon the stage
. . . how these pieces came to pass unpunished I do not know.'
(Lord MAHON's *Hist. of England*, ii. 232.) WALPOLE's enactment
is still in force.

¹⁰ *And strove in vain to laugh at H——y's jest.* This is sometimes given—*at Clodio's jest.*] At this time (1737) JOHNSON was well
acquainted with Mr. HENRY HERVEY, one of the branches of the
noble family of that name, who had been quartered at Lichfield as
an officer of the army, and had at this time a house in London,
where JOHNSON was frequently entertained, and had an opportunity
of meeting genteel company . . . and he described this early friend
HARRY HERVEY thus : ' He was a vicious man, but very kind to
me. If you call a dog *Hervey*, I shall love him.' (BOSWELL's *Life
of Johnson*, ch. iii.)

¹¹ *Who shares Orgilio's crimes.*] Orgilio is a personification for
the pride of wealth.—Fr. *orgeuil.*

¹² *All Marlborough hoarded.*] The Duke of MARLBOROUGH died
June 16, 1772. ' If we were to estimate his moral worth by his
double treachery to James II. and to William III., by his tame
submission to the ingratitude of Queen Anne, and *by the avarice
which degraded his private habits*, he might justly be numbered
among the greatest and meanest of mankind.' (*Eng. Cyclopædia,
Biography*, MARLBOROUGH.)

The Duke left his widow in possession of enormous wealth, inso-
much that she was able in some degree to control the public loans,
and affect the rate of interest. (Lord MAHON's *Hist. of England*,
vol. ii. 28.)

¹³ *All Villiers spent.*] GEORGE VILLIERS, Duke of Buckingham,
second son of George Villiers, Duke of Buckingham, who was as-
sassinated by Felton at Portsmouth, August 24, 1628, was born
1627. He was educated at Cambridge, and on the outbreak of the
civil war, espoused the Royalist cause. After the battle of Worcester
he fled abroad, but returned and married a daughter of FAIRFAX in
1657. CROMWELL arrested him, and committed him to the Tower.
On the abdication of RICHARD CROMWELL, he was released from
Windsor Castle, whither he had been removed. He became the
boon companion of Charles II., and was remarkable for the profligacy

of his moral and the versatility of his political conduct. ' He was a man indeed,' to use the strong language of a contemporary by whom he was well known, ' who had studied the whole body of vice. Notwithstanding his public and private crimes, he still retained the King's favour, and was employed on important embassies. But on the dissolution of the CABAL Ministry and his dismissal from office, he gradually weaned himself from the Court. He, however, spent the remainder of his days in factious opposition and in connection with the intrigues of Shaftesbury.

One incident in BUCKINGHAM'S life but too plainly exhibits the demoralisation of the times on which he was thrown. BUCKINGHAM having been detected by the Earl of Shrewsbury in an intrigue with his wife, killed him in a duel, while the wife of the unfortunate Earl held the Duke's horse during the combat in the disguise of a page. For this murder (1667–68) the Duke received a royal pardon.

On the death of Charles II., the Duke of BUCKINGHAM, conscious that he would have a more difficult master in his successor, and finding his health ruined by a long career of vice and his fortune diminished by unbounded extravagance, retired to his seat of Helmsley, in Yorkshire, where he devoted himself to field amusements. His death occurred April 17, 1688, at the house of a tenant at Kirkby Moorside, after a few days' fever produced by sitting on the damp ground when heated by a fox-chase.

The picture of destitution so finely drawn by POPE in the third of his *Moral Essays* is greatly exaggerated. POPE notes : ' This lord, yet more famous for his vices than his misfortunes, after having been possessed of 50,000*l.* a year and having passed through many of the highest posts in the kingdom, died in 1687 in a remote inn in Yorkshire reduced to the utmost misery.' The Duke had not reduced himself to beggary, nor did he breathe his last in ' the worst inn's worst room.'

The character which DRYDEN has presented under the character of ZIMRI in *Absalom and Ahithophel* is by no means thus overcharged, and may be unhesitatingly received, not only on account of the fineness of its execution, but also the justice of its features.

The Duke was interred under a sumptuous monument in Henry VII.'s Chapel, Westminster Abbey.

14. *The common sewer of Paris and of Rome.*] Rome is put here for Italy. OLDHAM had also imitated the Third Satire of JUVENAL and applied it to London, all which performances concur to prove that great cities, in every age and in every country, will furnish similar topics of satire. Whether JOHNSON had previously

read OLDHAM'S imitation I do not know ; but it is not a little remarkable that there is scarcely any coincidence found between their performances though upon the very same subject, the *only* instances are in describing London as the *sink* of foreign worthlessness :

> *the common sewer*
> Where France does all her filth and ordure pour.
> OLDHAM.

> The common sewer of Paris and of Rome.
> JOHNSON.

And lower down :

> No calling or profession comes amiss,
> A *needy monsieur* can be what he please.
> OLDHAM.

> 'All sciences a *fasting monsieur* knows.'—JOHNSON.
> (BOSWELL'S *Life of Johnson*, ch. iii.)

[15] *Illustrious Edward*], alluding to the victorious career of EDWARD III. in France.

[16] *Or like a gibbet better than a wheel.*] The former being an English, the latter a French mode of execution. Breaking on the wheel was a barbarous mode of execution of great antiquity. It was used for the punishment of great criminals, such as assassins and parricides, first in Germany ; it was also used in the Inquisition, and rarely anywhere else, until FRANCIS I. ordered it to be inflicted upon robbers, first breaking their bones by strokes with a heavy iron club, and leaving them to expire upon the wheel (to which they had been fastened) A.D. 1515. (HAYDN'S *Dictionary of Dates*, 1857.)

[17] *All sciences a fasting monsieur knows.*] (See above 14).

[18] *And lisp the tale of Henry's victories.*] Alluding to the victory of Agincourt and glorious reign of HENRY V.

[19] *Admires their wondrous talents for the stage.*] The period of the Restoration was characterized by a fatal French influence over the drama, literature, and taste. The appearance of females on the stage is altogether a modern custom, which originated on the Continent, and was not generally adopted in this country till the reign of Charles II. Anne of Denmark, wife of James I., Henrietta, wife of Charles I., and ladies of noble family, sometimes filled parts in masques and court entertainments, but this was not a case of professional actresses. PRYNNE, in the *Histromastrix*, denounces the attempt made in 1629 to introduce, according to Continental custom,

Frenchwomen at the Blackfriars Theatre. This was the first appearance of professional females on the English stage. They were, however, females; and much difference of opinion prevails as to the first English actress. Mrs. COLMAN, wife of Mr. Edward Colman, appeared as *Ianthe*, in the *Siege of Rhodes in* 1656. PEPYS saw women on the stage for the first time January 13, 1662.

> 20 *Of all the griefs that harass the distressed,*
> *Sure the most bitter is a scornful jest.*]

The passage in JUVENAL,—

> Nil habet infelix paupertas durius in se
> Quam quod ridiculos homines facit—

is better translated by OLDHAM than by JOHNSON. OLDHAM'S translation, though less elegant, is more just—

> Nothing in poverty so ill is borne,
> As its exposing men to grinning scorn.

21 *No peaceful desert yet unclaimed by Spain.*] Pope ALEXANDER VI., at the beginning of the sixteenth century had assigned to Spain all lands discovered more than 473 leagues west of the Azores. The Spaniards at this time were said to make claim to some of our American provinces.

22 *And bear Oppression's insolence no more.*] (See above p. 17.)

23 *Some fiery fop with new commission vain.*] In illustration of the allusions JOHNSON makes to the social characteristics of the time, we may give a general picture of the condition of things then in town and country. [London was like all the large towns very dirty, and very badly protected. It abounded in open places, where were thrown and lay unremoved all the filth and refuse that was not cast into the gutter. Carriage-way and footpath were hardly distinguishable from one another.] The streets were lighted only in winter. At night they were protected by a few decrepit watchmen—were infested with robbers—and were frequented by the *fashionable young men about town*, and *officers as* JOHNSON suggests, whose great amusement was to insult and maltreat the passers-by, and to fight with drawn swords other parties of exquisites whom they might meet. Club and coffee house life formed a great feature of the metropolis: here politics, literary and theatrical matters, and the state of the funds were discussed.

The London merchants lived over their shops, which were marked by signboards instead of by numbers.

[The country gentlemen were as a rule ignorant, foul-mouthed, and their *summum bonum* of life in many cases consisted in drunkenness, good living, and unlimited sport. The country clergy were ill paid, and despised.] The sturdy yeoman, or small farmer class, continued to be numerous and powerful, and maintained the old English spirit.

Of the labouring classes, quite one half were farm-labourers.

One fifth of the population were paupers.

[Roads were bad and travelling was tedious; and carriages at night in London were attended by men who carried torches or flambeaux. Stage waggons and horses were the usual modes of conveyance for both passengers and goods. The roads were infested by highwaymen, but abounded in excellent inns.]

'A vast amount of disease and destitution existed in London and the larger towns. The prisons were in a disgraceful state. The Committee appointed to report upon their condition in 1729 found in the sick wards of some of the gaols emaciated objects lying on the floors without beds and actually dying of starvation.

[24] *Such crowds at Tyburn die.*] This celebrated place of execution, first established in the reign of Henry VI., is derived from a brook called Tyburn, which flowed down from Hampstead into the Thames, supplying in its way a large pond in the Green Park, and also the celebrated Rosamond Pond in St. James's Park. Oxford Street was at an earlier period known as *Tyburn Road*, and the now aristocratic locality of Park Lane bore formerly the name of *Tyburn Lane*, whilst an iron tablet attached to the railings of Hyde Park, opposite the entrance of the Edgware Road, informs the passer-by that here stood *Tyburn turnpike-gate*, so well known in old times as a landmark by travellers to and from London.

The gallows at Tyburn was of a triangular form, resting on three supports, and hence it is often spoken of as '*Tyburn's triple tree.*' It appears to have been a permanent erection; but where it actually stood is a matter of controversy; most probably at the end of Connaught Place where it joins the Edgware Road and nearly opposite the entrance to Upper Seymour Street. A lane led from Uxbridge Road to the place of execution.

Curious documents called *Tyburn tickets* were certificates conferred under an Act passed in the reign of William III. on the prosecutors who had succeeded in obtaining a capital conviction of a criminal. The object of this was to stimulate individuals in bringing offenders to justice. The document exempted the holder from serving in all manner of parish and ward offices. The tickets were transferable, and sold like other descriptions of property. This Act was repealed in 1818 ; but a claim for exemption from serving on a jury on the strength of a Tyburn ticket was made as late as 1856.

The conveyance of criminals from Newgate to Tyburn was by Holborn Hill and the Oxford Road. A court on the south side of the High Street, St. Giles's, is said to have derived its name of *Bowl Yard* from the circumstance of criminals on their way to execution being presented at the Hospital of St. Giles with a large bowl of ale as their last refreshment. (CHAMBERS'S *Book of Days,* ii. 557.)

HARRISON'S '*Description of Great Britain,*' printed in 1577, states that 72,000 rogues and thieves suffered death in the reign of Henry VIII.—that is about 2,000 a year. And at this time ' Hanging-day' came round regularly ; in one year 97 malefactors were executed in London, and 20 on one morning. There is no wonder at this if we remember that in the reign of George II. *sixty-three* capital offences were added to the Statute Book, making a total of 120 *crimes punishable by death.*

[25] *To rig another convoy for the king.*] The frequent visits of GEORGE II. to his Continental possessions and his protracted absences made him exceedingly unpopular. In 1736 there was great exasperation and much popular indignation on this account, which found vent in *pasquinades.* In December the King came home after public hopes rather than fears had been excited by the belief that he was at sea during a terrible storm in which many ships had been wrecked. (See KNIGHT'S *Pop. Hist. Eng.* vi. ch. 5.)

[26] *In Alfred's golden reign . . . . no special juries known.*] ALFRED'S reign was a mythical *golden age* with many poets and historians. Juries, neither common, nor special, existed then for the simple reason that though traces of trial by jury are found in the reigns of William I. and II. Henry I., and Stephen, it was not fully established until the reign of Henry II.

Trial by Jury was first adopted in criminal cases in the reign of John, and was the established mode of dealing with them at the end of the thirteenth century.

'*THE VANITY OF HUMAN WISHES.*'

¹ O'erspread with snares the clouded maze of fate.] The future of our lives made more difficult by the dangers from temptations to which we yield.

² Impeachment stops the speaker's powerful breath.] Since the beginning of the century there had been the following cases of impeachments : (1715) Bolingbroke, Oxford, and Ormond for their share in the *Peace* of Utrecht. (1725) Lord Chancellor Mansfield was impeached for peculation, found guilty and fined 30,000*l.* From the circumstances of the time we can well understand that the threat was often used, and the idea of it familiarised.

⁵ And leaves the wealthy traitor in the Tower.] In 1720 the crash of the South Sea Bubble took place. A Committee of the Commons was appointed to investigate the proceedings of the company. Amongst those implicated in receiving bribes were the Duchess of Kendal, and Madame de Platen, (sister to the Countess of Darlington), Sunderland, Craggs, AISLABIE and several members of Parliament. Sunderland was acquitted by the House, Craggs died during the enquiry, AISLABIE was expelled from Parliament and sent to the Tower, with the confiscation of a great part of his property.

⁴ The needy traveller, serene and gay,
Walks the wild heath and sings his toil away.|

So CHAUCER, *Wyf of Bathes Tale* :

> Juvenal saith of poverty merily,
> The pore man, when he goth by the way
> Before the theeves he may synge and play.

The wild tracks about London, especially Hounslow Heath, were infested with highwaymen.

⁵ gaping heir],—*anxiously awaiting the succession to his wealth and fortune.* Alluding to Frederick, Prince of Wales.

⁶ Democritus.] The 'laughing philosopher' was born at Abdera, in the 80th Olympiad. His claim to the title of *Laugher* (ὁ γελασῖνος) has been disputed, and by moderns generally rejected. Perhaps the native stupidity of his countrymen afforded him incessant matter for laughter. Perhaps he was by nature satirical, and thought ridicule the test of truth. We have no proof of his being a *satirist*,

F

except the tradition ; that may be false, but must have had some
origin.

DEMOCRITUS was of a noble and wealthy family, so wealthy
that it entertained Xerxes at Abdera on his return from Asia.
Xerxes in recompense left some of his Magi to instruct the young
Democritus. Most of the tales handed down about him are idle,
such as, the fact of his having put his eyes out with a burning glass
in order that he might be more perfectly undisturbed in the exercise
of his reason. Respecting his philosophy, we have more certain
evidence ; but even that has been so variously interpreted and is
in many parts so obscure that historians have been at a loss to give
it its due position in relation to other systems. He taught that our
truth is only the truth of impression, not the truth of fact, and set
himself to solve the grand problem—*How do we perceive external
things?* His system was a decided advance on that of his pre-
decessors, and made very decided progress in two great points of
Psychology and Physics. (See LEWES' *Biog. History of Philosophy.*)

7 *A new made mayor's unwieldly state.*] In the days of William
the Conqueror this office was called a *Port reeve* ; in the days of
Henry I. a *Justiciar* ; in a Charter of Henry II. he is called *Mayor.*
from the Norman *maire.* In olden times the Mayor was elected
on the Feast of the Apostles Simon and Jude (October 28), and it
was customary for him on the day of his election to go on foot by
land, or by boat on the river Thames, to be sworn into office at
Westminster. The title—Lord—was added to Mayor in 1354.
The procession was converted into a pageant in 1454 by Sir John
Norman, who proceeded to Westminster in a barge.

8 *That hung the bright palladium of the place.*] Ancient
authors give different traditions respecting the origin of this
celebrated statue of Pallas or Minerva, some stating that it fell from
heaven, during the building of Ilium, others that it fell at Pessinus
in Galatia, others that Electra gave it her son Dardanus, and others
that it was merely an ingenious automaton ; but all agree that the
fate of Ilium depended on its preservation. Its capture consequently
became a great object with the Greeks during the siege, and it was
stolen by Ulysses and Diomede B.C. 1183. Other authorities state
that only a fictitious statue was stolen, and that the real *palladium*
was conveyed into Italy by Æneas, B.C. 1181, and was preserved
with great secresy in the Temple of Vesta. Elagabalus attempted to
carry it off in 219, but a counterfeit image was substituted for it.
The Roman Palladium was a small statue three cubits and a half in

height, and it was kept in a barrel, and placed near other barrels to
prevent theft. ('TOWNSHEND'S *Manual of Dates.*)

⁹ *But will not Britain hear the last appeal.*] (See supra the
story of Jenkins's ear—*London,* page 57.)

¹⁰ *Through Freedom's sons no more remonstrance rings,*
Degrading nobles, and controlling kings.]
On November 22, 1641, PYM presented to the House of Commons
the Grand Remonstrance on the state of the kingdom.

This was a *severely elaborate review* of the misgovernment of
CHARLES I. in church and state from the beginning of his reign.
It consisted of 206 articles, condemnatory of the King's acts, was
debated during seventeen hours in the House of Commons, and
carried by a majority of eleven. This had been preceded by the
attainder of STRAFFORD, and was followed by the impeachment of
twelve bishops, and the arrest of Laud, the visit of Charles to the
House of Commons to arrest the five members, the discontent in
London, the flight of the King, and the Civil War.

¹¹ *Septennial ale.*] The Septennial Act was passed in 1716.
Under the Act passed in 1694, the duration of Parliament had
been fixed at three years. The cause of that narrow limitation
may probably be found in the enormous period of seventeen years
to which Charles the Second had prolonged his second Parliament,
and which by a natural revulsion drove the minds of men into the
opposite extreme.

The cause which principally influenced Ministers in passing the
Septennial Act was a case of pressing and immediate danger. A
rebellion (the Pretender's attempt, 1715) scarcely quelled—an inva-
sion still threatened—parties in the highest degree exasperated—a
government becoming unpopular even from its unavoidable
measures of defence; such were the circumstances under which
the Parliament, according to the Act of 1694, was about to be dissolved at the risk of tumults and bloodshed, a most formidable opposition, and perhaps a Jacobite majority.

Under these circumstances the Septennial Bill was passed to
avoid the dangers of the situation by postponing a dissolution of
Parliament. (vide Lord MAHON'S *History of England,* vol. i.
200.)

¹² *In full blown dignity see Wolsey stand.*] THOMAS WOLSEY,
the son, as was said, of a butcher of Ipswich, having received a
learned education, entered the Church. He became tutor in the
family of the Marquis of Dorset, who, pleased with his talents, re-

commended him to Henry VII., by whom he was made one of the
royal chaplains. The king employed him in a secret negotiation
respecting his marriage with Margaret of Savoy, and was so pleased
with him in it, that he bestowed on him the deanery of Lincoln. Soon
after the accession of Henry VIII., WOLSEY was made Almoner,
a situation which brought him into constant intercourse with the
King ; and the polish and gaiety of the Almoner's manners, and the
readiness with which, though in orders and nearly forty years of
age, he entered into the royal pleasures—even, it is said, singing,
dancing and carousing with the youthful courtiers, quickly won him
the heart of Henry, who was also aware of his talents for business,
and delighted with his skill in the theology of the schools. Prefer-
ments rapidly flowed in upon him. On the taking of Tournay he
was made bishop of that see ; he then became Dean of York, then
Bishop of Lincoln, and finally Archbishop of York within one year
(1514). He was now courted by foreign princes, and even the
Pope, to secure his influence, sent him a cardinal's hat (1515) ; and
the same year, on the resignation of Archbishop Wareham, the
King conferred on him the office of Chancellor. The Pontiff finally
(1518) invested him with the dignity of Papal Legate, and his ambitious mind now aspired even to the Papacy itself.

The wealth of WOLSEY was enormous. Besides his archbishopric,
he farmed the revenues of the sees of Hereford and Worcester,
which were held by foreigners ; he held *in commendam* the Abbey
of St. Albans, and the see of Bath, which he afterwards exchanged
for the see of Durham, and this again for the more wealthy see of
Winchester. His legatine court and the chancery brought him in
large emoluments, and he had pensions from the Pope, the Emperor,
and the King of France. Bound to celibacy by his order, profuse
and vain by nature, he hoarded not his wealth. He lived in a style
of princely magnificence, and barons and knights were among the
officers of his household : palaces, abbeys, colleges rose or were
enlarged by his munificence. The learned men of all countries
tasted of his bounty. At the same time in his office of Chancellor
he was just and upright, and his improvements in the administration
of justice entitled him to the gratitude of the people.

13 *At length his sovereign frowns.*] The frown which presaged
WOLSEY's downfall came in 1529. In that year, after long en-
deavours made with the Pope to obtain a court to try the question
of Henry's divorce with Catherine of Arragon, Cardinal Campeggio
and Cardinal Wolsey his assessor were obliged to open the Legat-

me Court, from which Henry sanguinely expected a decision in his favour. The court broke up without pronouncing judgment, and the matter was transferred to Rome, whither Henry and Catherine were both cited to appear. The King's anger at this disappointment fell upon WOLSEY, who, with the whole body of the Church, was visited with the penalties for having violated the Statute of Præmunire.

At Michaelmas, WOLSEY was deprived of the Great Seal, his immense property was confiscated, and he himself was ordered to reside in his diocese of York. A short time after removing thither, he was arrested by the Duke of Northumberland on a charge of high treason ; and, whilst travelling to London, he was seized with a dysentery, and died at the Abbey of Leicester, November 28, 1530.

[14] *What gave great Villiers to the assassin's knife.*] (See above, *London,* page 59, note 13.)

[15] *And fixed disease on Harley's closing life.*] ROBERT HARLEY, Earl of Oxford (1661-1724), was descended from an ancient family in Hereford. At the time of the Revolution, Robert and his father raised a troop and took possession of Worcester for the Prince of Orange. On the accession of William, he supported the Whigs in the House of Commons, but afterwards passed over to the Tories. Thrice he was elected to the Speaker's chair. In 1704 he was made Secretary of State, and resigned four years later in consequence of the treason of one of his clerks. On the fall of the Whigs in 1710, HARLEY was appointed Chancellor of the Exchequer, and the year following created a peer. Shortly after, he was created Lord Treasurer, and held the post till within three days of the close of the reign. For his part in the Treaty of Utrecht he was impeached in 1715. After two years' imprisonment in the Tower, he was discharged. The Earl of Oxford survived his imprisonment in the Tower seven years. He was a great patron to literature, and spared no pains or expense in collecting printed books and valuable manuscripts. This collection of manuscripts was purchased by Parliament (26 Geo. IV). and forms the well-known HARLEIAN Collection in the British Museum.

[16] *What murdered Wentworth.*] THOMAS WENTWOTH, Earl of Strafford, flourished 1593-1641. He was educated at Cambridge, sat in two Parliaments in the reign of James I. In 1627 he was imprisoned for refusing to pay to a forced loan, and spoke out boldly against the public grievances. Soon after he accepted the overtures of the Court, and was made Baron Wentworth—then he became President of the Council of the North, and a Privy

Councillor. Sent over to govern Ireland, his government was marked by oppressive severity. In 1640 he was summoned to England, made Earl of Strafford, impeached by Pym, and beheaded May 12, 1641. Macaulay says : ' He employed all his powers for crushing those liberties of which he had been the most distinguished champion. His counsels respecting public affairs were fierce and arbitrary. In Ireland, where he stood in the place of the King, he set up the authority of the executive over that of the courts of law.'

[17] *What exiled Hyde.*] EDWARD HYDE, Earl of Clarendon (1608–74), was educated at Magdalen College, Oxford, and the Middle Temple. He entered Parliament in 1640, took part against Strafford, but soon after, displeased at the violence of the Parliamentary proceedings, he gave support to the Court. Charles now made him one of his counsellors. He fled from England in 1645, and was one of the principal adherents and advisers of Charles II. At the Restoration he rose to be Chancellor, but his haughtiness and temper produced a general dislike which ended in his impeachment. When in exile he moved about from place to place, till he died at Rouen. His private character was good, his public one not sufficiently firm and courageous. Hyde's daughter married James II.

[18] *O'er Bodley's dome his future labours spread.*] The small original University Library, Oxford, had been completely despoiled, and in 1556 even the fittings of the room over the Divinity School were sold. In 1551 THOMAS BODLEY, Esq., sometime Fellow of Merton, resolved to restore the Library, and secure it by an endowment of land. In 1602 the library was again opened with more than 2,000 books. In 1617, the founder, who had been knighted by James I. made extensive additions to it, and left his property for this purpose.

[19] *And Bacon's mansion trembles o'er his head.*] There is a tradition that the study of Friar Bacon, built on an arch over the bridge, will fall when a man greater than Bacon shall pass under it. To prevent so shocking an occurrence it was pulled down many years since. (JOHNSON's note.)

ROGER BACON, the Franciscan friar, flourished at Oxford about 1214–92. By his devotion to physical science he gained the reputation of a sorcerer. His *Opus Majus* is an enquiry into the roots of wisdom,— viz., language, mathematics, optics, and experimental science.

[20] *To buried merit raise the tardy bust.*] This refers to SAMUEL BUTLER, the author of the *Hudibras.* The rapid success of this

poem brought BUTLER under the notice of the Court, whose interests the satire had so powerfully served. CHARLES II. presented the author with 300*l*., promising to do more for him. This promise the King never fulfilled; and the great wit, after living in poverty or obscurity for a few years longer died in 1680 in a wretched lodging in Covent Garden, then the most miserable and squalid quarter of London. He was even indebted to the charity of a friend for a grave. Sometime after his death, he received the honour of a monument. This tardy recognition of BUTLER'S merit gave origin to one of the acutest epigrams in the English language :—

> Whilst Butler, needy wretch, was yet alive,
> No generous patron would a dinner give,
> See him, when starved to death and turned to dust
> Presented with a monumental bust :
> The poet's fate is here in emblem shown,
> He asked for bread and he received a stone.

[21] *Hear Lydiat's life.*] The history of LYDIAT being little known, the following account of him may be acceptable to many of my readers. It appeared as a note in the Supplement to the *Gentleman's Magazine* for 1748, in which some passages extracted from JOHNSON's poem were inserted, and it should have been added in the subsequent editions.—' A very learned divine and mathematician, Fellow of New College, Oxon, and Rector of Ockerton near Banbury. He wrote among others a Latin treatise *De Naturâ Cæli*, &c. in which he attacked the sentiments of SCALIGER and ARISTOTLE, not bearing to hear it urged, *that some things are true in philosophy and false in divinity.* He made above six hundred sermons on the *Harmony of the Evangelists.* Being unsuccessful in publishing his works, he lay in the prison of Bocardo, at Oxford, and in the King's Bench, till Bishop Usher, Dr. Laud, Sir William Boswell, and Dr. Pink released him, by paying his debts. He petitioned King Charles I. to be sent into Ethiopia to procure MSS. Having spoken in favour of monarchy and bishops, he was plundered by the Parliamentary forces, and twice carried away prisoner from his rectory, and afterwards had not a shirt to shift him in three months without he borrowed it, and died very poor in 1646. (BOSWELL'S *Life of Johnson.*)

[22] *Galileo's end.*] GALILEO, was the son of a Florentine nobleman, and was born at Pisa 1564. At the age of twenty-four he

became Mathematical Professor at Pisa. He was obliged to resign his professorship in 1592, and went to Padua. There he invented a telescope, and with it he made some remarkable astronomical discoveries, Jupiter's satellites, Saturn's rings, the Sun's spots, and the starry nature of the Milky Way. Hence he championed the Copernican system. Twice he was brought before the Inquisition, in 1615 and 1633. On both occasions he was compelled to abjure the Copernican system. Milton visited him in prison in 1638. He was afflicted with blindness, and died in prison in 1642 from the effects of a slowly consuming fever. This was the year in which Sir I. NEWTON was born. (See HALLAM's *Hist. of Literature,* ch. viii.)

23 *Rebellion's vengeful talons seize on Laud.*] JOHNSON's high Tory principles naturally led him to consider the civil war between King and Parliament as a *great rebellion*—such as Clarendon terms it.

WILLIAM LAUD, the son of a Berkshire clothier, was born at Reading. In 1589 he entered St. John's College, Oxford, of which he became a Fellow and ultimately President. Next from Chaplain to King James he became Dean of Gloucester, then Bishop of St. David's. In 1628 he was removed to London, and became Primate in 1633. His administration was fatal to Charles and himself, and the severities of the Star Chamber made him detested. He was executed 1643.

24 *The plundered palace.*] This has reference to Whitehall. We still possess the Parliamentary order permitting 'Mr. John Milton,' Latin Secretary of the House of Commons, to 'choose and take away such hangings as he thinks fit, from the dismantled palace of Whitehall. Scott's novel of *Woodstock* gives a picture of scenes that took place there and elsewhere in the country.

25 *The sequestered rent.*] *Sequestrations* were first introduced by Sir NICHOLAS BACON, Keeper of the Seals to Queen Elizabeth, and father of Lord Bacon. Commissioners, called *Sequestrators,* were appointed, whose province it was to discover and punish by fine any favourers of Royalty.

26 *Gazette's pompous tale.*] The first English Gazette was published at Oxford, the Court being there then on account of the plague November 7, 1665. On the removal of the Court to the capital, the title was changed to the *London Gazette,* February 5, 1666. *London Gazettes Extraordinary* are used for the publication of extraordinary official news. One of these latter was forged with a

view of affecting the funds May 22, 1787. The fraud succeeded, and the perpetrators of it were never discovered. (HAYDN's *Dictionary of Dates.*)

[27] *And stain with blood the Danube and the Rhine.*] This has reference to the battles &c., fought by MARLBOROUGH, such as the *Siege of Bonn,* battles of *Hochstadt* and *Donauwerth;* the campaign on the Rhine in 1734, and the battles of Dettingen and Fontenoy in 1743 and 1745.

[28] *From age to age in everlasting debt.*] The present national debt commenced in the reign of William III. It had amounted in 1697 to 5,000,000*l.* In 1749, the date of this poem, to 78,000,000*l.* In 1856 it was nearly 800,000,000*l.* Since that time it has been reduced.

[29] *How just his hopes let Swedish Charles decide*]. CHARLES XII. of Sweden succeeded to the throne at the age of fifteen, in 1697. When he was eighteen, a league was formed against him by Frederic IV., the King of Denmark, Augustus, Elector of Saxony and King of Poland, and Peter I. of Russia, the object of which was to dismember Poland. Charles attacked Copenhagen, and in a few weeks forced the King of Denmark to sue for peace. He then defeated the Russians at Narva. Next he turned his arms against King Augustus. Ultimately he deposed him, and Stanislaus became King of Poland instead. Charles then invaded Russia, and ultimately laid siege to Pultowa, where the Russians had collected great stores. Peter the Great arriving to relieve it, Charles risked a general battle, which ended in the defeat of the Swedes. Charles took refuge in Turkey, and the Sultan, Achmet III., assigned him a liberal allowance and the town of Bender on the Dniester. In 1714 Charles left Turkey, and, without going to Stockholm, immediately took the field against Prussia, Denmark, Saxony, and Russia. He was obliged to return to Sweden in 1715. In 1716 he invaded Norway; and again in 1718, when besieging Fredericshall in the midst of winter, he was killed by a musket ball.

[30] *Behold surrounding kings their powers combine.*] Peter the Great; Frederic IV. of Denmark ; Frederic Augustus, King of Poland and Elector of Saxony.

[31] *One capitulate.*] The King of Denmark in 1700.

[32] *And one resign.*] The King of Poland in 1701.

[33] *Hide Pultowa's day.*] The battle of Pultowa was fought on July 8, 1709.

[34] *A petty fortress and a dubious hand.*] FREDERICSHALL, on

the coast of Norway. It has been a matter of controversy whether CHARLES was struck by an enemy's bullet or one from some treacherous hand among his own friends.

³⁵, ³⁶ *The bold Bavarian in a luckless hour.*] This alludes to the war of the Austrian Succession, in which England was concerned, 1741-1748. CHARLES VI. of Austria, having no male heir, ordained the *Pragmatic Sanction*, by which a female was made eligible to succeed to the Austrian dominions. By virtue of this, on Charles's death in 1740, his daughter Maria Theresa succeeded him.

CHARLES ALBERT, Elector of Bavaria, put in a claim to the throne, and was supported by France and Spain. England supported Maria Theresa with 300,000*l.* and 12,000 men.

Frederic the Great of Prussia took advantage of circumstances to put in a claim to parts of Silesia. He invaded it, and defeated the Austrians at Molwitz. A French army invaded Bavaria, proclaimed the Elector Duke of Austria, and under him marched into Vienna. He was shortly after crowned King of Bohemia at Prague, and then elected Emperor at Frankfort.

³⁷ *Tries the dread summits of Cæsarean power.*] He aspired to be Emperor.

³⁸ *Fair Austria spreads her mournful charms,*

   The queen, the beauty, sets the world in arms.] The fair Archduchess of Austria—MARIA THERESA—on the approach of the Elector and the French to Vienna, fled to Hungary. At Pesth she addressed the Magnates in their Diet, who drew their swords and responded with the shout, *Moriamur pro nostro rege, Maria Theresa.*

³⁹ *The wild Hussar.*] ·The word Hussar is an Hungarian term, and really applies to the light horsemen of that country, whence it was imported into other European armies. (see GLOSSARY, page 79.)

⁴⁰ *The baffled prince in honour's flatt'ring bloom*

   Of hasty greatness, finds the fatal doom ;

   His foes' derision and his subjects' blame,

   And steals to death from anguish and from shame.] At this juncture (1745) an event happened which seemed to insure success to the projects of Maria. CHARLES (the Elector of Bavaria), who was naturally of an infirm constitution, was worn out by grief at the depression of his own fortunes and the sufferings of his exhausted country. Though restored to a temporary possession of his capital, he was in hourly apprehension of being again driven from the seat of his ancestors, and reduced to a precarious dependence on France.

In this state of alarm and anxiety, he was afflicted with a severe attack of the gout, when one of his domestics officiously related the defeat of a French and Bavarian corps at Neunec, which was aggravated by their dastardly behaviour. This sudden communication of a disastrous event affecting the sensitive mind of the unfortunate monarch, the disorder remounted to his stomach and proved fatal. Charles expired at Munich, January 20, 1745. (COXE'S *Hist. of House of Austria,* iii. 306.)

[41] *From Marlborough's eyes the streams of dotage flow.*] Two domestic trials were the cause of the affliction which overtook the Duke of MARLBOROUGH in the last years of his life. One was the death of the young Marquis of Blandford, a blow which the Duke felt sorely. Another bereavement he suffered on March 22, 1714, by the premature decease of his daughter, Lady Bridgewater, in the twenty-sixth year of her age. Marlborough refused to be comforted. He withdrew to the retirement of Holywell, and there became first afflicted by that melancholy distemper under which first his mind and eventually his body sunk. . . On May 28 he was smitten with paralysis, but under skilful treatment he gradually recovered his strength. But he never wholly recovered his articulation, nor the full power of his memory. He went to Bath, and returned in a certain degree to society, resuming with apparent ease the ordinary course of his employment. That his faculties were not absolutely impaired, is demonstrated by the fact that it was subsequently to this, his first seizure, that he played his part on the trial of Lord Oxford, while he realised 100,000*l.* by his successful speculation in South Sea Stock. But it seems an idle as well as an uncalled-for perversion of truth to contend that from his first attack he ever was the man he had been previously. If the 'tears of dotage' did not flow from his eyes, it is certain that much of the vigour of mind which once belonged to him was lost, and even his speech continued embarrassed in the pronunciation of certain words.' (GLEIG'S *British Military Commanders,* vol. ii. 216.)

[42] *And Swift expires a driv'ler and a show.*] During the whole of his life, SWIFT had been grievously afflicted with attacks of deafness, giddiness and pain in the head ; and his gloomy and despondent spirit seems to have looked forward with prophetic dread to insanity as the probable termination of his existence. An affecting anecdote is related by Dr. YOUNG of SWIFT having been found mournfully gazing on a noble oak, whose upper branches had been struck by lightning—' I shall be like that tree,' said SWIFT, ' I

shall first die a-top.' Nor were these melancholy predictions falsified by the event. About the year 1736 he was attacked by repeated fits of pain, and loss of memory, and in the composition of that terrific invective, the *Legion Club*—he was seized by a species of fit from whence he never recovered sufficiently to finish the poem. The long and melancholy interval of nine years intervening between this time and his death was one uninterrupted succession of mental and bodily suffering. He passed from a deplorable and furious mania to a state of idiotcy ; and the active politician, the resistless polemic, the satirist, the poet, and the wit died, as he himself had feared and half predicted, 'in a rage, like a poisoned rat in a hole.' This event took place October 19, 1745, at Dublin. (SHAW's *Outlines of Literature*, 286.)

⁴⁵ *Yet Vane could tell what ills from beauty spring.*] In this poem, a line in which the danger attending on female beauty is mentioned has very generally I believe been misunderstood :—

Yet Vane could tell what ills from beauty spring.

The lady mentioned here was *not* the celebrated LADY VANE whose memoirs were given to the public by Dr. Smollett, but ANNE VANE, who was mistress to Frederick Prince of Wales, and died in 1736, not long before JOHNSON settled in London. Some account of this Lady was published under the title of *The Secret History of Vanella*, 8vo. 1732. In Mr. BOSWELL's *Tour to the Hebrides* (p. 37. fourth edition) we find some observations upon this and the following line :—

⁴⁴ *And Sedley cursed the form that pleased a king.*] Lord HAILES told JOHNSON he was mistaken in the instances he had given of unfortunate fair ones, for neither VANE, nor SEDLEY, had a title to that description. His lordship therefore thought that the lines should have run thus—

> ' Yet *Shore* could tell—
> And *Valière* cursed—'

Our friend, he added in a subsequent note addressed to Mr. BOSWELL on this subject) chose VANE, who was far from well looking, and SEDLEY (mistress of James II.) who was so ugly, that Charles said, 'his brother had her by way of penance.' (Note by MALONE, BOSWELL's *Life of Johnson.*)

GLOSSARY.

————◦◦◦————

AMBUSH. Ital. *bosco*, Fr. *bois*, a bush, wood ; Fr. *embuscher*, to go into a wood or thicket, thence to lie in wait.

ASSASSIN. *Hashish* is the name of an intoxicating drug, prepared from hemp, in use among the natives of the East. Hence Arab. *Haschischin*, a name given to the members of a sect in Syria, who wound themselves up by doses of *Hashish* to perform at all risk the orders of their lord, known as the Sheik or Old Man of the Mountain. As the murder of his enemies would be the most dreaded of these behests, the name of *assassin* was given to one commissioned to perform the murder. (WEDGWOOD's *Dict. of Etymology.*)

ATTORNEY. Mod. Lat. *attornatus*, one put in the *turn*, or place, of another ; according to Blackstone's definition, 'who is put in the place, stead, or turn of another to manage his matters of law.'

AWKWARD. In its present signification, unhandy, maladroit ; which yet is by no means its earlier. There is good reason to think that the same Ang.-Sax. *aweg* appears equally in the first syllable of 'awkward' and 'wayward.' The *awk* end of a rod is the *away* end. 'What makes matter say they, if a bird sings *auke* or crow-cross?' Holland, *Livy*, p. 247. (TRENCH's *Select Glossary.*)

BIER. Ang.-Sax. *Bæran*, to bear, that which bears the corpse : so (Wiclif, Luke vii. 14) 'And he came nygh and touchide the *beere*.'

CANOPY. Mod. Greek, κωνωπείον, a mosquito curtain, from κώνωψ, a gnat.

CANVASS. Lat. *cannabis*, hemp. To canvass a matter, is a metaphor taken from sifting a substance through canvass.

CELL. Lat. *cella*, a store-room, a place for depositing grain or fruits.

DARKLING. This is no participle of the verb *to darkle*, but an adverb of derivation like *stillenge*=secretly (Med. High-German) : so blindlins, backlins, darklins &c. in Lowland Scotch. (LATHAM'S *Eng. Language*, vol. ii. 318.)

May not ' ling ' be the common diminutive suffix? thus the word whilst an adverb would signify whilst a little dark, at twilight, as in the expression of Milton, *the nightingale sings darkling.*

DOTARD. Dutch, *doten, dutten, delirare, desipere*, to dote, rave, be foolish. (WEDGWOOD, *Dict. of Eng. Etym.*) The termination ' ard ' is augmentative—one of the two we possess, ' ard ' and ' oon,' as dotard—balloon.

DISSIPATED. Literally scattered here=spent in dissipation.

DEBAUCHED. Fr. *débauche. Bauche*, a course of bricks in a building, hence *desbaucher*, to throw out of order. (WEDGWOOD, *Dict. of Etym.*) Trench favours the derivation from Bacchus, Lat. *debacchari*, to revel like a bacchanal, Fr. *debaccher*. (RICHARD-SON'S *Dictionary.*)

FARM. Ang.-Sax. *feorm*, a supper, board, hospitality; *feormian*, to supply with food. The modern sense of farm arose by degrees. In the first place, lands were let on condition of supplying the lord with so many nights' entertainment for his household. Thus the Saxon Chronicle, A.D. 775, mentions land let by the Abbot of Peterborough on condition that the tenant should pay 50*l.* and *anes nichtes feorme*, i.e. one night's entertainment. Then, of course, payment in kind gradually changed to money payment. (WEDG-WOOD'S *Dict. of Eng. Etym.*)

GAUDY. Lat. *gaudium*, joy.

GAZETTE. Commonly derived from *gazzetta*, a small Venetian coin, supposed to have been the price of the original newspaper ; but the value of the coin was so small that it could never have paid for a written or printed sheet. The true meaning of the word is shown in the Ital *gazzetta*, all manner of idle chattings or vain prattlings, now used for running reports, daily news, &c. The origin of the word is a representation of the chattering sound of birds : Ital. *gazza*, a magpie ; *gazzettare*, to chatter as a pie or jay. (WEDGWOOD'S *Dict. of Eng. Etym.*)

GIBBET. Fr. *gibet*, Ital. *giubette*, a halter ; then used for the framework from which a man was hung.

GROOM. Dutch, *grom*, a youth ; Goth. *guma*, A.-S. *gym in*, to attend ; O.-S. *bridegumo*, bridegroom. Whether -*r*- has been inserted in one case or lost in the other we cannot say. (WEDGWOOD, *Dict. of Etym.*)

GULLED, duped, metaphorically taken from the stupidity of the sea-mew. Ital. *gulone*; Welsh, *gwylan*, from the peculiar wailing cry of the bird (W.).

HERMIT, or eremite, from ἐρῆμος, a desert. One who dwells alone in the desert.

HIND. A word corrupted in sound from A.-S. *hine*, a servant.

HUSSAR. Hungarian, a light horseman ; *husz*=twenty and *ar*=pay. Every twenty houses furnished one cavalry soldier.

JAIL. Ultimately derived from Lat. *cavea*, a cave or cellar, but GOAL, from *caulis*, a stem or pole round which the charioteer drove.

LENITIVE, from *lenire*, to assuage.

MASSACRE. Commonly derived from O.-F. *macecrier*, a butcher; Lat. *macellus*, a meat market.

MADDED, i.e. maddened, *en* as a suffix makes a verb causative, thus madden = to make mad.

MAIN. Literally powerful, mighty, chief, principal ; so main, i.e. main sea, main-land, main-mast ; A.-S. *magan*, to be able. In composition *main* signifies great.

METROPOLIS. μήτηρ and πόλις = the mother city.

MIMIC. Gr μῖμος ; Lat. *mimus*; a farcical entertainment or the actor in it, hence an imitator.

MOTLEY. 'Motley life.' *Motley* originally meant a habit composed of various colours, the customary dress of a domestic fool.

Invest me in my *motley* ; give me leave to speak my mind.
As you like it, ii. 7.

' Men of motley ' is equivalent to ' fools.'

OSIER. Fr. *osier*, a willow, willow twig, wicker basket.

PARASITE. Gr. παράσιτος ; Lat. *parasitus*; one who takes food (σῖτος) with another.

PLUNDER, Dutch, *plonderen*. The word is supposed to have been introduced into England at the commencement of the Great Rebellion.

PREY. Lat. *præda*, booty.

RANSACK. A.-S. *ran* ; rapine, plunder, and *secan*, to seek = to seek for plunder.

SECURE, i.e. *sine curd*.

SYCOPHANT. Gr. Συκοφάντης, from indicting persons that exported figs, an informer ; an informer of anything pleasing to the hearer ; a flatterer, a parasite. 'They say they did forbid in the old time that men should carry figs out of the country of Attica ; and that from thence it came that those pick-thanks which betray and accuse them that transported figs were called *sycophants.* (RICHARDSON, *Eng. Dict.*)

TRANSMUTE. A word borrowed from Alchemy, which aimed at changing baser metals into gold.

VASSAL. 'Feudatory or *vasal* was only another name for the tenant or holder of the lands, though on account of the prejudices which we have justly conceived against the doctrines grafted on this system, we now use the word *vasal* opprobriously as synonymous to slave, a bondman.' BLACKSTONE.

Low Lat. *Vassus* is derived from *vas*, a pledge of surety. The vassals were undoubtedly tenants upon pledge, to render certain services to their lord.

WHERRY, may be from A.-S. *faran*, to go ; but others take it from *werian*, to weary.

WOUD. An error for would. Would and should are proper, but in cou*l*d the *l* is inserted by a false analogy from the example of would and should. The word should be *couthe* or *coud* : not so *woud*, to remove the *l* from which would be wrong.

PRINTED BV
SPOTTISWOODE AND CO., NEW-STREET SQUARE
LONDON

www.ingramcontent.com/pod-product-compliance
Lightning Source LLC
Chambersburg PA
CBHW020309090426
42735CB00009B/1278